Tino Rangatiratanga
me te Kāwanatanga
*Government and Organisation*

# Sovereignty versus Rangatiratanga: Wars, Laws and Policies

**Wars, Laws and Policies**
**1st Edition**
**Ruth Naumann**

Cover design: Macarn Design
Text design: Macarn Design
Production controller: Siew Han Ong

Any URLs contained in this publication were checked for currency during the production process. Note, however, that the publisher cannot vouch for the ongoing currency of URLs.

© 2022 Cengage Learning Australia Pty Limited

**Copyright Notice**
**Copyright:** This book is not a photocopiable master. No part of the publication may be copied, stored or communicated in any form by any means (paper or digital), including recording or storing in an electronic retrieval system, without the written permission of the publisher. Education institutions that hold a current licence with Copyright Licensing New Zealand, may copy from this book in strict accordance with the terms of the CLNZ Licence.

For product information and technology assistance,
in Australia call **1300 790 853**;
in New Zealand call **0800 449 725**

For permission to use material from this text or product, please email **aust.permissions@cengage.com**

**National Library of New Zealand Cataloguing-in-Publication Data**
A catalogue record for this book is available from the National Library of New Zealand.

978 0 17 046241 9

**Cengage Learning Australia**
Level 7, 80 Dorcas Street
South Melbourne, Victoria Australia 3205

**Cengage Learning New Zealand**
Unit 4B Rosedale Office Park
331 Rosedale Road, Albany, North Shore 0632, NZ

For learning solutions, visit **cengage.co.nz**

Printed in Singapore by C.O.S. Printers Pte Ltd.
2 3 4 5 6 7 26 25 24 23 22

**Acknowledgements**
Cover: *Death of Major Von Tempsky at Te-Ngutu-o-te-Manu, New Zealand, 7th September, 1868,* Watkins, Charles Henry Kennett, 1847-1933; Archibald Dudingston Willis (Firm); Potts, William, 1859-1947, C-033-006, Alexander Turnbull Library.

Shutterstock for images on pages 6, 7, 8, 10, 19, 52, 99, 100, 117, 123, 124.

iStock for images on pages 11, 12 (Marriage Customs), 16, 20, 29, 38 (lower), 40, 57 (top), 49, 83, 111, 112, 114, 115.

NZ Post for images on pages 7, 18.

Chris Slane, Slane Cartoons Ltd, for the cartoons on pages 116 and 121.

Auckland Art Gallery for painting Frank Wright, Walter Wright, *The Canoe Builders*, 1915, oil on canvas, 1099 x 1911 mm, Auckland Art Gallery Toi o Tamaki, gift of Mr C J Parr, 1915, Accession No 1915/5 on page 13.

Otago University Research heritage for page 110, *An incident during a Hauhau raid on a settler's farm.* Painted by Major von Tempsky. Presented by Mrs N Kettle (née von Tempsky).

Alexander Turnbull Library for images on page 4, Makaenuku Pa, E-070-007 (Brees, Samuel Charles, 1810?-1865; Melville, Henry, 1792-1870); page 24, John Rutherford, A-090-028 (Dempsey, John Church, 1802-1877, Docker, Alfred, -1930?; Docker, Conrad Eley, 1895?-, Fox, Charles Arundel Overbury (Dr), 1886?-1971); page 21, Russell (Kororareka) from Watering Bay, A-234-010 (Mesnard, Theodore Romuald Georges, 1814-1844); page 23, Oihi Bay, Christmas Day 1814; Samuel Marsden preaching the first sermon to the Maoris, B-077-002 (Morgan, Jack, active 1961-1966; Weekly News); page 24, Henry and William Williams calming hostile Maori by speaking extracts of the Bible in Maori, PUBL-0151-2-013 (artist unknown); page 26, Flotte de guerre. Nouvelle-Zeeland. A-442-050 (Sainson, Louis Auguste de, 1800-; Danvin, Victor Marie Felix, 1802-1842; page 27, Portrait of Edward Parry, a baptized New Zealand youth, 1834, E-296-q-180-2; page 28, Etablissement des missionaires (Nouvelle Zelande). B-052-019 (Sainson, Louis Auguste de, 1800-; Arago, Jacques Etienne Victor, 1790-1854); page 33, Captain William Hobson G-826-1 (McDonald, James Ingram 1865-1935); page 34, A reconstruction of the signing of the Treaty of Waitangi, 1840, A-242-002 (Mitchell, Leonard Cornwall, 1901-1971); page 38, Head and shoulders portrait of a young Maori man, wrapped in a blanket. He was Maketu Waretotara, the son of Ruhe, a Waimate chief, E-216-f-011 (Merrett, Joseph Jenner, 1815-1854); page 39, Settlement of Wellington by the New Zealand Company. Historical gathering of pioneer ships in Port Nicholson, C-033-005 (Clayton, Matthew Thomas, 1831-1922); page 47, *H M S North Star, destroying Pomare's pa, Otiuhu, Bay of Islands* (1845), A-079-032 (Williams, John, -1905?; Bridge, Cyprian, 1807-1885); page 48, *The war council.* June 1864, A-159-047, (Tempsky, Gustavus Ferdinand von, 1828-1868); page 51, Rangihaeta, Te Raparaha's fighting general and chief actor in the Wairau Massacre, A-114-046 (Hall, R, active 1840s; Coates, Isaac, 1808-1878); page 53, *Heke fells the flagstaff at Kororareka*, A-004-037 (McCormick, Arthur David, 1860-1943); page 54, *The warrior chieftains of New Zealand*, C-012-019, (Merrett, Joseph Jenner, 1815-1854; page 56, Okaihou, A-079-029 (Williams, John, -1905?); page 57, Ruapekapeka, N.Z. 1846,A-079-030 (Williams, John, -1905?; Bridge, Cyprian, 1807-1885); page 58, Ohaiawai 1st July 1845, A-079-028 (Williams, John, -1905?); page 59, Makaenuku Pa, E-070-007 (Brees, Samuel Charles, 1810?-1865; Melville, Henry, 1792-1870); page 63, The invasion of Auckland by the Ngatipaoa, April 17th, 185, C-033-003 (Wilson & Horton); page 64, Te Werowero, or Potatau the principal chief of all Waikato, PUBL-0014-44 (Angas, George French, 1822-1886); page 65, Troops of the 40th Regiment being ferried ashore by lighters from H. M. S. Victoria, C-030-013 (Harris, Edwin, 1810?-1895); page 66, *Storming the Waireka Pah, Taranaki*, PUBL-0098-02-24-06-lower; page 69, Deviation on the road to Waikato, made by the Royal Artillery, through Williamson's Clearing, PA1-q-250-48; page 73, *Attack on the Maori Pah at Rangiriri.* PUBL-0046-4-39 (Redmayne, Thomas, active 1880s-1890s); page 74, *The fight at Rangiaohia for the recovery of McHale's body.* February 21 1864. Colonial Defence Force; page 77, *"Ake! Ake! Ake!" Rewi defying the British troops at Orakau,* C-033-004, (Wilson & Horton lith. Auckland, Wilson & Horton, 1893); page 80, View of the trenches at Gate Pa, Tauranga, A-033-007 (Robley, Horatio Gordon, 1840-1930); page 88, page 104, Te Ua Haumene, who founded the Hauhau Church. Taken by an unknown photographer in the 1860s, 1/2-005495-F; page 89, Pai Marire karakia at Tataroa, New Zealand, to determine the fate of their prisoners. Jan[uar]y 27th, 1865,
B-139-014 (Meade, Herbert George Phillip, 1842-1868); page 100, Armed Constabulary, Gisborne, PAColl-1767-1; page 102, Portrait of Rua Kenana. Taken by James Mcdonald in 1908.1/2-019618-F; page 104, Erueti Te Whiti-o-Rongomai III - Sketch made by William Francis Robert Gordon, PA1-o-423-10-4; page 104 and 105, Parihaka Pa, Taranaki, 1/1-013095-G, PA1-q-183-19, (William A Collis); page 106, *The New Native Policy.* The New Zealand Punch [Wellington], 27 March 1880; page 108, Moreu, Michael, *He iwi tahi tatou*, 6 February 2015, DCD-0031090; page 119, Tame Iti holding pou whenua, accompanied by Whina Cooper, leading Maori Land March along Hamilton street, taken 26 September 1975 by Christian Heinegg on the leg between Ngaruawahia and Kihiki, 35mm-87527-2-F.

Museum of New Zealand, Te Papa Tongarewa for images on page 45, New Zealand Company / United Tribes flag, 1839, maker unknown. Gift of Andrew Haggerty Richard Gillespie, 1967. CC BY-NC-ND 4.0. Te Papa (GH002925); page 42, *Storming of the Pa at Ruapekapeka, 11th January 1846,* New Zealand, by John Williams. Purchased 2000 with New Zealand Lottery Grants Board funds. Te Papa (2000-0008-1); page 49, *Untitled (Army camp)*, 1860s, New Zealand, maker unknown. Purchased 1999 with New Zealand Lottery Grants Board funds. Te Papa (O.020480); page 62, *Interior of a native village or "pa" in New Zealand.*, circa 1852, by John Gilfillan. Gift of Horace Fildes, 1937. Te Papa (1992-0035-1744); page 67, *View of Mt Egmont, Taranaki, New Zealand, taken from New Plymouth, with Maoris driving off settlers' cattle*, 1861, Melbourne, by William Strutt. Purchased 2015. Te Papa (2015-0042-1); page 90, Rev. C. S. Volkener, circa 1900, by William Francis Gordon. Purchased 1916. Te Papa (O.013574); page 91, *Savage dance, Pai Marire - Volkner's death*, March 21st, 1865, PUBL-0033-1865-47-080-2 (Illustrated London News); page 92, General Chute K.C.B. O.012369/02; page 93, *On General Chute's march, West Coast*, 1992-0035-1186, (Major Gustavus von Tempsky; artist; circa 1868); page 96, Sections of Taurangaika Pa, John Buchanan; surveyor; circa 1868; page 99, Maori rebel flag: Flag of Te Kooti, 1870, 1992-0035-1631/2, Gift of W.F. Gordon, 1916;

The National Library of Australia for image on page 15 Landing of Captain Cook in New Zealand by Edwyn Temple.

Auckland Libraries, Sir George Grey Special Collections, for image on page 86.

Public domain images, page 9, Chatham Islands people, 1910; page 12, The Legend of the Voyage to New Zealand, Kenneth Watkins, 1912; page 22, The blowing up of the *Boyd* by Louis John Steele (1889); page 28, James Busby as a young man painted in Sydney 1831 or 1832; page 32, A pencil sketch of Charles Philippe Hippolyte de Thierry by an unknown artist; page 36, The Waitangi Sheet of the Treaty of Waitangi, signed between the British Crown and various Maori chiefs in 1840; page 37, Imperial Federation, map of the world showing the extent of the British Empire in 1886; page 43, from *Bush Fighting. Illustrated by remarkable actions and incidents of the Maori War in New Zealand ... With a map, plans, and woodcuts ...*, by Alexander, James Edward – Sir; page 44, Auckland 1857, (John Hursthouse); page 61, View of Whanganui, New Zealand, 1847, (JA Gilfillan), State Library of New South Wales; page 68, The Volunteers at Waireka. NZ Illustrated Magazine, 1903; page 70, Queen's Redoubt Pokeno; page 71, Albert Barracks, Auckland, N.Z., with Mount Eden in the distance (John Williams); page 72, *The Attack on the Pukekohe East Church Stockade, 1863,* (from a drawing by A. H. Messenger); page 72, Waikato River Gunboat; page 78, 1895 British book *Illustrated Battles of the Nineteenth Century*; page 79, Henare Taratoa: a chief of the Ngai Te Rangi tribe, Watercolour by H.G. Robley, 1864. Wellcome Collection; page 81, A Maori exodus, New Zealand, illustration from the magazine The Illustrated London News, volume XL, February 1, 1862; page 84, Image captured by the Moderate Resolution Imaging Spectroradiometer (MODIS) on NASA's Aqua satellite; page 87, Airini Donelly, The rural economy and agriculture of Australia and New Zealand; page 95, Portrait of the Maori leader Titokowaru (Illustrated Australian News for Home Readers); page 97, Taking a Maori redoubt / McFarlane & Erskine (Blair, David, 1820-1899); page 103, *Maungapohatu*, photo by George Bourne. Auckland Institute and Museum; page 107, King Tawhiao by the artist Gottfried Lindauer; page 108, Queen Victoria of England by the artist Alexander Melville.

Tino Rangatiratanga me te Kāwanatanga
*Government and Organisation*

# Sovereignty versus Rangatiratanga: Wars, Laws and Policies

RUTH NAUMANN

# Contents

# 1 Pacific Setting

**Historians understand that because Polynesian ancestors of Māori are the first to arrive and settle, Māori history is the beginning and continuous history of people in Aotearoa New Zealand.**

New Zealand is in Te Moana-nui-ā-Kiwa – the Pacific Ocean. It is the largest body of water on the planet. So big that all the continents could sit in it and there would still be room for more. Te Moana-nui-ā-Kiwa is one of the last areas that humans explore and settle. The last big bit of land outside the Arctic and Antarctic in which humans settle is New Zealand. It is located in the part of the Pacific called Polynesia.

The people who discover New Zealand and first settle in it are Polynesian. Polynesians have a tight relationship with Te Moana-nui-ā-Kiwa. They find islands in it long before Europeans see them. When people settle on islands, they make cultures, ways of living, that are special for each island. At the same time the different cultures have things they share. An example is Māui, the trickster hero who captures the sun, fishes up islands, turns into a bird and goes into the underworld in search of his father. Another example is language. When English explorer Captain James Cook visits New Zealand, he has a priest called Tupaia from Tahiti on board his ship. Māori, who are descendants of the Polynesians, cannot understand Cook. But they understand much of what Tupaia says.

*Kupe.*

Some oral traditions say the great Polynesian chief Kupe is the first arrival in New Zealand. Perhaps he lands in Hokianga Harbour about 800 years ago where he lives for about 40 years? Different iwi have different details about Kupe. Some say he is not the first to arrive, that people greet him. He iwi atua, supernatural fairies, live in forests and mountains. They are rarely seen as they move about only in dusk and night or thick mist. One tradition says Kupe's competitor has a pet octopus which takes fish and bait from lines. Kupe sets out in a waka to kill it. He chases it all the way to Raukawa (Cook Strait) and kills it. Some traditions say his wife Hine-te-Aparangi (sometimes called Kuramārōtini) sees New Zealand and thinks it is a long white cloud. He Ao! she cries. He aotearoa!

The Pacific is the highway for Polynesians. Their double-hulled waka have sails and outriggers. They are fast and easy to manage, even in rough water. They carry food and water. Some are up to 36 metres long. The *Endeavour*, the British sailing ship of Captain Cook, is about 32 metres long.

Pacific means peaceful but imagine being in such waka when a storm blows up and all around are monster waves. Historians do not know how many waka are lost at sea. They do know that Polynesian sailors have to be brave and skilful. Their navigators have to be ultra-observant. For example, they will see that long-tailed cuckoos spend winter in the tropical Pacific islands in the north. But in winter the birds fly south. The observers will know that there is land to the south. The people move around the Pacific by watching nature – rising and setting points of sun, moon, stars; sky colours and clouds; behaviour of birds and fish; water, waves, currents; wind direction; how the waka feels on the water. Historians think these Polynesians arrive in Aotearoa between 1200 and 1300. They are the first settlers, the indigenous people, the first known in a place. They become tangata whenua, people of the land.

## Mahi Skills

1 **Local history:** There may be local history experts in your school – ākonga, kaiako. Along with iwi and hapū they hold local history. Learning about your local area is said to be getting to know where your feet are. Decide how you might try setting up a relationship with local experts.

2 **Close reading:** Read the following and think about how you might use ideas to contribute to a discussion about what history is.

> History is a taonga. Some people say it should be written as *hi story* as it is all about stories. Māori and non-Māori can have different approaches to history. Māori hold their history in ways that include whakapapa, te reo Māori, waiata, whakataukī, rote learning, karakia, tradition, kōrero, kōrero pūrākau, hui, mihi, tukutuku, recital. They know that many answers to a question can be right, that hapū and iwi and whenua have different traditions. A non-Māori approach is to write history down and try to find a single history for all hapū and iwi and whenua. Sometimes books begin with the so-called discovery (more on that in Chapter 5) of New Zealand by Europeans, which means a lot of early history is missing.

3 **Mapping:** Make a sketch map of the world and label continents, oceans, Polynesia and New Zealand.

4 **Collaging:** Put the word Culture in the middle of a page. Add its meaning. Add drawings or pictures or text about your culture around it.

5 **Assessing:** Footprints of Kupe is in Opononi on the Hokianga Harbour. Find out about it and assess the things you might learn from it. Assess the best way to get to it from your place and how long it would take.


PHOTOCOPYING OF THIS PAGE IS RESTRICTED UNDER LAW.
ISBN: 9780170462419

# Moriori Myth 2

**Historians know about myths. One meaning of myth is traditional story. Ancient tribes in Europe who are ancestors to many Pākehā created myths to explain their world. Their myths about monsters and spells and love affairs may have inspired modern stories such as Harry Potter. Another meaning of myth is a widely-held but untrue idea. Historians bust these.**

New Zealand has a Moriori myth. It concerns the Chatham Islands (Wharekauri in Māori), which are part of New Zealand. They are about 800 km east of the South Island. The myth says that once upon a time, New Zealand has a race of people called Moriori. Polynesian people arrive. They are stronger and smarter than Moriori. They kill and eat Moriori. They take over their land. The facts tell a different story. Moriori are indigenous people of the Chathams. They arrive there about 1500. Probably from mainland Aotearoa rather than straight from Polynesia but nobody knows for sure. They are Polynesian. They develop a culture that is different in some ways to Māori culture developing in Aotearoa. For example, they say no war, no killing, no eating of human flesh.

Why does the myth come about? Historians suggest one reason could be that when Pākehā believe Māori are dying out in the late 19th century, it is good to have a story about another race dying out because of Māori. Another theory is that Pākehā use it to justify colonisation in Aotearoa — that if Māori colonise Moriori then the British can do it to Māori. Another theory links it to those Māori traditions that say there are people in Aotearoa when their ancestors arrive. And later there actually is a Māori-Moriori violent confrontation. During the musket wars when iwi fight iwi in New Zealand, Ngāti Mutunga and Ngāti Tama from Taranaki lose land. They move down to Te Whanganui-a-Tara — Wellington. In 1835 they hijack a ship and force it to take women, men, children, seed potato, pigs, waka, guns, clubs and axes to the Chathams. On 19 November and 15 December 1835 two groups totalling about 900 arrive. Moriori take the visitors in and look after them until groups of armed Māori warriors begin to takahi or walk the land to lay claim to it. You are now slaves, they tell Moriori. We have taken possession of the land in accordance with our custom.

*Moriori family in about 1910.*

Chatham Islands (Wharekauri).

The Moriori decide to keep their policy of not fighting, even when Māori begin to attack and kill. You cannot marry Moriori, have children with Moriori or speak Moriori, Māori say. They keep Moriori as slaves until 1863. By this time the population has gone from about 1700 in 1835 to about one hundred. And by this time New Zealand is in the midst of the New Zealand Wars.

## Mahi Skills

1 **Local history:** Find out how Moriori chief Nunuku-whenua and Tommy Solomon fit in with local history of Wharekauri.

2 **Understanding emotive terms:** Some people today talk of the Moriori genocide. Genocide is an emotive term because it arouses so much emotion. Find other emotive terms. An example is holocaust, which an MP uses in a maiden speech in the New Zealand Parliament.

3 **Putting events in context:** Context is the time and environment in which events take place. Today it may seem strange that Māori can hijack a ship and load it up without alerting authorities. Aotearoa is very much a Māori country in the 1830s and the Wellington area is nothing like it is today. Find images and descriptions of it at that time.

4 **Understanding power:** Understanding that power means ability to influence events and people will help you understand all Aotearoa New Zealand history. Explain how power is used in the Māori-Moriori relationship.

5 **Geography:** Make a copy of the map and learn the approximate locations of the areas named.

# New Whenua 3

**Historians show how Polynesian migration brings traditional ideas of knowledge and knowing that is today called mātauranga Māori. In Aotearoa the links with land and sea stay strong. Central to a developing value system is tikanga – a way of organising behaviour to create balance and good actions.**

Imagine climbing off a waka and gazing about. No houses. No tracks, no roads. A land of birds. Including the Haast eagle, the largest eagle ever. And the moa – no wings so it will be easy to hunt. A huge place to explore. Forest, bush, mountains, rivers, lakes. The people will need to create technologies, build fortified pā and unfortified kāinga (villages). Life will be tough. Constant physical work can cause arthritis. Grit in food wears down teeth. The average life expectancy is about 28 to 30 years, the same for much of Europe at the time.

In this new land of seemingly endless resources, they cut down and burn forests for bird-hunting, crops, settlements, bracken to grow so their roots provide food. They witness the last moa, last Haast eagle, last goshawk, last adzebill, last of some duck species. They cause numbers of seals, sea lions, elephant seals to go down. Birds have no learned defence against the Polynesian rat. It almost wipes out tuatara.

Over time they develop kaitiakitanga – care for the environment. Leave enough tuatua for the bed to survive, they teach tamariki. Don't set traps while birds are breeding. How people behave towards the environment and each other is related to tapu – ancestral power, the non-ordinary. People, places, objects, events that are tapu are not to be messed with. It is bad to disrespect tapu, such as fishing in a cove that is tapu because someone recently drowned there, until it is made noa – ordinary. Mana is also about people and environment. A person with mana has energy and authority, is respected, is not going to collapse when things get rough. Everyone can get, and lose, mana from actions.

*Everywhere, the new settlers begin a human history and relationship with the land, water, animals and plants.*

Utu is about keeping things balanced. More about restoring harmony than getting revenge. It is linked to the exchange of gifts, which can be a form of barter, so people get goods they cannot provide themselves. A gift of kūmara from an inland hapū to a coastal tribe, and much later, maybe after a rangatira has dropped a hint, a gift of dried fish to the inland hapū. A gift such as a piece of pounamu, or a kindness such as a feast, sets up an obligation to give in return. It does not have to be immediately. It might be much later. If a person insults another, the insulted one looks to balance things so mana is made whole again. A taua (war party) might set off to get utu. Or the wronged person might take something as compensation (this action is called muru) from the offender.

The people have an oral culture. They record their history in words that will be recited down the generations. They have a common language although each iwi has its own dialect or special form.

## Mahi Skills

MARRIAGE CUSTOMS.—NEW ZEALAND: MODE OF DECIDING BETWEEN RIVAL SUITORS.

1 **Local history:** Each area has its own tikanga. List places or people you might approach to learn about this.

2 **Establishing accuracy:** This image (at right), described as Māori marriage customs, appears in the 19th century at a time Europeans are interested in cultural practices different to their own. Find out how accurate the image might be.

3 **Demonstrating:** Explain how you would demonstrate the differences between an oral and written culture.

4 **Problem-solving:** Write out what you think the term mana Māori means.

5 **Identifying an image:** Work out what this action directed at an early European settler is about.

PHOTOCOPYING OF THIS PAGE IS RESTRICTED UNDER LAW.
ISBN: 9780170462419

# Rangatiratanga 4

**Historians understand terms. They know rangatiratanga means chieftainship, leadership, chiefly authority and know it relates to ideas about power, rule, control, organisation.**

A bird flying upwards will see how people arrange themselves into groups in the new land. Firstly, a small group. A whānau, extended family. It has wharepuni (sleeping houses) in the kāinga, and behind it are its resources – a plot in the kūmara garden, a special hunting place.

Higher up the bird can see that the whānau, along with others, is part of a hapū. The most important political unit. It has its own rangatira and controls a piece of territory. It can have one or several kāinga. The bird can see the boundaries of hapū are rivers, hills, piles of stones. Very high up the bird can see how various hapū make up an iwi – a tribe spread over a large territory. It looks like a nation – people who are separate from other iwi who are out of sight. The iwi governs itself through rangatira. The most powerful and high-ranking chief is the ariki. The other out-of-sight iwi do their own thing.

Every individual in these groups has a relationship with Papatūānuku, Mother Earth who gives birth to all. It provides tūrangawaewae – a place to stand. For everyone, from that toddler taking its first steps to this kaumātua directing tamariki fetching water in gourds. They share land with ancestors, living and unborn. It goes back to Polynesian ancestors finding a place to put feet down and stand after waka voyages. However, people are mobile. They move with seasons. Over there is a group walking to a bird-snaring place. They will be away for a while.

*Tohunga are specialists in skills such as healing, tattooing, carving and building. This group will have a tohunga waka-building expert. The group can possibly smell smoke in the air from ahi kā fires which show continuous occupation of people keeping fires going to cook kai.*

This land gives this iwi, hapū and whenua identity. Ko au te whenua, ko te whenua ko au – I am the land and the land is me, they say. Rangatiratanga is authority over land. It is held by groups, not individuals. This woman here has just had a baby. The pito (umbilical cord) and whenua (placenta) are buried. The woman and her baby belong to this land and have rights on it. But they do not own it for themselves.

The people do not use money and do not see land as something to be bought or sold. A gifting of land, or rights such as access to a fishing ground, is a most valuable gift. They name features as a way of recording history. Like the names of their groupings such as Ngāi Tūhoe (people of Tūhoe), Te Whānau-ā-Apanui (family of Apanui), Ngāti Manawa (ancestor killed by spear through heart).

It is not always this peaceful. Imagine that last month two hapū worked together to store food for winter. But now there is a rūnanga in one of the hapū. A taua is to be formed. Has someone in the other hapū given an insult, or committed an assault or adultery? Murder? How bad will it be – will they want to obliterate the enemy, reduce some to kai to take away mana? Or will it be enough to kill a few only and then withdraw? Whatever happens, it will be controlled by rangatiratanga. A tohunga may sprinkle water as purification and strengthening on warriors with knotted and feathered hair and faces with red ochre and charcoal marks. They will fight with hand-to-hand weapons such as taiaha, patu and mere made of stone and wood. They will make a peace at the end. Perhaps an arranged marriage between winning chief and high-ranking female of the losing hapū. The winners will increase their mana and maybe also gain resources. Maybe the losers will have to migrate away.

## Mahi Skills

1 **Local history:** Write down at least five place names, Māori or English, from your area and try to find their origin. Place names can store history and so correct spelling is important.

2 **Understanding meaning of key (of great importance):** A key element in rangatiratanga is land. Give some examples to show this.

3 **Understanding whanaungatanga (sense of belonging):** Show how whanaungatanga is connected to rangatiratanga.

4 **Defining:** Make a list of at least ten terms from this chapter and give a brief definition for each one.

5 **Planning a graphic novel page:** Plan a page for a graphic novel to show the following.

> The battle of Hingakākā at Lake Ngaroto in Waikato in the late 18th century is said to be about the largest ever fought in New Zealand. One day rangatira Pikauterangi from Kawhia visits Waikato. At a feast, he takes offence. Is it because of the amount of fish he is given? He spends three years gathering a war party of up to 10,000–16,000 warriors. Locals, who number less than half that, have a warning system of alarms and learn Pikauterangi is on the way. They gather at Taurangamirumiru pā. Waikato iwi win the battle. Along with many of his warriors, Pikauterangi is killed. Many others drown in wetlands and swamps. The name Hingakākā refers to the many high-ranking chiefs who fall (hinga) that day, slain in great numbers like parrots (kākā).


PHOTOCOPYING OF THIS PAGE IS RESTRICTED UNDER LAW.
ISBN: 9780170462419

# Rangatiratanga Meets Sovereignty

5

**Historians look at the relationship between beliefs and actions. When the European Age of Exploration brings explorers, including Dutchman Abel Tasman in 1642 and Englishman James Cook in 1769 to Aotearoa, two different approaches to governing and organisation with all their different beliefs meet head-on.**

Europeans say they discover New Zealand even though when they arrive people are already there. The land is new to Europeans but to people living on it Europeans are visitors. Europeans also name places that Māori have already named. A bay west of Mangonui in Northland is said by some to be where Kupe first lands. In December 1769 James Cook and Frenchman Jean de Surville are on ships in this area at the same time although they do not see each other. Cook has already sailed by this bay and named it Doubtless Bay. Less than two weeks later de Surville anchors in the bay and calls it La Baie de Lauriston in honour of a Governor of French India. Māori have known the beach there as Tokerau for a long time.

On 6 October 1769 Cook's ship, the *Endeavour*, is off the east coast of Te Ika-a-Māui (North Island). The surgeon's young helper, Nicholas Young, sees Te Kurī-a-Pāoa, a headland at Tūranganui-a-Kiwa. He will be super-proud when Cook calls it Young Nick's Head. He does not know that Māori living there have an ancestor named Kiwa from Tākitimu waka and that a tradition says Kiwa waits so long for the Horouta waka to arrive he calls its final landing place Tūranganui-a-Kiwa — long waiting place of Kiwa.

Cook's party brings pigs.

A Dutch mapmaker calls the country that Tasman has seen Nieuw Zeeland. Zeeland is a Dutch province. Later Cook translates the name into English – New Zealand. And what have Māori been calling it? Experts suggest the North Island is Te Ika-a-Māui (the fish of Māui) and the South Island is Te Wai Pounamu (rivers of greenstone) but Māori do not use one name for both. Later, the Māori version of a document uses Nu Tīreni for New Zealand, and another uses Nu Tirani. Aotearoa usage is thought to have increased about the time of the New Zealand Wars in the 19th century and flags used by some warriors are said to have Aotearoa on them. When the national anthem of 1878 is translated into Māori, Aotearoa is used for New Zealand. This helps spread the idea among Māori and Pākehā that Aotearoa means all of New Zealand.

Why do Europeans claim and name land like this? Europe has a law about discovery. The Pope, who has a lot of political power in Europe, issues this law. The law suggests that when Europeans arrive at lands which already have indigenous people, it is okay for Europeans to claim the land. They believe God favours Christian lands such as England, Spain, France, Italy as being superior to non-Christian lands such as Pacific islands. Indigenous people are inferior and the land they live on is terra nullius – nobody's land. Christian explorers can therefore claim it in the name of their sovereign. Today, such ideas go by names including white supremacy and are said to be against human rights. When Europeans first see New Zealand, people do not think of or talk about human rights. They have accepted the law about discovery without question.

Both Tasman and Cook are given written instructions by their bosses. Tasman's includes ...

*You will prudently prevent all manner of insolence and all arbitrary action on the part of our men against the nations discovered, and take due care that no injury be done them in their houses, gardens, vessels or their property, their wives ...*

Cook's includes ...

*To exercise the utmost patience and forbearance with respect to the natives ... To check the petulance of the sailors, and restrain the wanton use of firearms ... shedding the blood of those people is a crime of the highest nature.*

Servant, Pope, Sovereign.

Cook is often described as being an honourable man with good intentions. When he arrives in Aotearoa, the British are building the largest empire and navy the world has ever had. They do this by taking over places they sail to. This is colonisation. Like Tasman's visit, his first visit ends up with some dead sailors and some dead Māori. When New Zealand in 2019 commemorates his first visit, not everyone wants to celebrate.


PHOTOCOPYING OF THIS PAGE IS RESTRICTED UNDER LAW.
ISBN: 9780170462419

Christopher Columbus 'discovering' the Americas.

Cook's bosses do not give him a manual labelled Māori Rangatiratanga and Tikanga. And Māori have no knowledge of British beliefs which include Christian values of hard work and discipline, individual ownership of houses and land, centralised government in London's Parliament and monarch, strict punishments, gender inequality, that colonisation is good for the colonised, that colonies are useful for providing trade opportunities and making money. This is a recipe for what is called Cultural Misunderstanding. One example is what British see as trading or bartering, Māori see as gift exchanging. When Māori do not hand over goods immediately, British see dishonesty to be punished. Māori, used to gift exchanging which might take months to work out, see strangers giving them gifts and then attacking them.

What must locals make of ships and crews that suddenly appear at their place? Floating islands? Giant birds? Atua? Non-waka, with strangers in red and white, come to the shore; why backwards? And what about that smell? Locals do not yet know that sailors live rough. No hot baths with soap, no flush toilets, no deodorant, no fresh water to wash clothes.

Locals light fires of warning in the hills. Warriors are ready. Do they blow shells to challenge the visitors and scare them off? Do they think the visitors are patupaiarehe, maybe coming to take women and children? Do they try to protect kūmara gardens? Do they get nervous because visitors anchor too close to the cave of a taniwha and so threaten to wake up its spirit; do the visitors arrive in the middle of a hui or tangi? Do locals have spears for a wero welcome and then see a stranger lift a long stick that makes a loud noise and causes a chief to fall down dead?

During Cook's first visit, Māori meet a man dressed in long boots, coat and breeches who can talk to them. He is Tupaia from Tahiti who knows some English. A priest with star navigation as his speciality. He visits the *Endeavour* in Tahiti and decides to go with it when it leaves. Cook is not happy with this but botanist Joseph Banks thinks Tupaia will make a good curio – something unusual to be displayed. Māori will remember Tupaia better than Cook and see the *Endeavour* as Tupaia's ship. He is connection with their history and can calm tense situations. When Cook lands at Motuarohia Island many Māori are there so maybe it is a pōwhiri and haka that scares Cook's men into shooting at and wounding Māori who cross a line Cook draws in the sand. A story says that later Tupaia visits and treats a shot chief who gives Tupaia a carved whale tooth pendant and bone heru (comb). When Cook comes back three years later with news of Tupaia's death, Māori are saddened. It is Tupaia they want to see again. Not Cook.

## Mahi Skills

*1940.*

1 **Local history:** Explain why different hapū and iwi will have different histories about their first contact with or hearing about Europeans.

2 **Primary and secondary sources:** Historians view material prepared at the time of an event, such as Tasman and Cook writing about what Māori look like, as primary sources. Material prepared by people who are not around at the time of the event, such as a painting done a hundred years after Cook's visit, is a secondary source. Explain which type of source the instructions (page 16) are and why.

*1992.*

3 **Seeing change:** A 1940 stamp issued is called Tasman's discovery of New Zealand 1642 and one in 1992 is called Sighting of New Zealand Tasman 1642. Describe the change and give a reason for it.

4 **Digging deeper:** Find answers for the following. Cook's second voyage of 1772–75 has two ships which get separated and Cook has arranged that if that happens they should head for Ship Cove (Meretoto). What happens to sailors sent off in a boat to collect wild greens and how does Cook react? Another explorer who comes to New Zealand, in 1772, is Frenchman Marion du Fresne. How and why does he die?

5 **Using criteria (standards by which something or someone is judged):** Decide if James Cook breaks his instructions by doing the following. He gives English names to places that already have Māori names. His crew kill nine Māori in 1769. Even though he struggles with the idea of kaitangata, eating people, he writes, *'They eat their enimies slane in Battel – this seems to come from custom and not from a savage dispossission ...'* He makes the first recorded circumnavigation of New Zealand, and puts New Zealand on maps of the world. He punishes crew members who steal from Māori. He sees Māori as noble, smart, artistic, brave, open, warlike.


PHOTOCOPYING OF THIS PAGE IS RESTRICTED UNDER LAW.
ISBN: 9780170462419

# Relationships 6

**Historians look at relationships, how they develop and perhaps change. European explorers writing about Aotearoa's resources – fresh water and food, timber, flax, seals, whales, and souls to save – matches European consumer demand. Now Aotearoa is no longer closed off from the rest of the world.**

Hundreds of people come to Aotearoa, especially to resource-rich Te Pēwhairangi (Bay of Islands) where Kororāreka is the first permanent European settlement. It is busy and noisy and missionaries call it the hellhole of the Pacific because they do not approve of its grogshops, its visiting whalers and traders looking for female companionship, its escaped convicts and deserting sailors. Relationships are not always smooth. Ship crews take fresh water, timber, fruit, fish, birds. Maybe they do not understand that Māori have customary rights and re-gifting is needed. They go into kūmara gardens, camp in tapu places, use whare that look abandoned but are not. Young Māori with spear-throwing skills are good harpooners and some join whaling ships. If the captain treats them badly, there may be a need to get utu to restore balance.

Some visitors write accounts. Joseph Price, a sealer, tells of a night-time raid when Māori set fire to huts, skins and provisions, tie up the sealers' hands and march them towards Fiordland. Nothing to eat but roasted fish, says Price. Until they are fed flesh taken from captives. Survivors escape and a ship picks them up.

Some visitors settle among Māori and have Māori wives and children. Traders Dicky Barrett and Jacky Love form a relationship with Te Āti Awa at Ngāmotu (New Plymouth). They have Māori wives and in 1832 help Te Āti Awa beat off a Waikato attack. John Rutherford, who goes to sea when he is ten, later arrives on a whaling ship. Māori kill some crew but adopt John. He gets tattooed, learns te reo Māori and is made a chief. Charlotte Badger, shipped off to be a convict in New South Wales, escapes with a group of male convicts and they take over the ship. Charlotte, it is said, dresses as a man and flogs the captain. The mutineers drop her off at Rangihoua in the Bay of Islands. Charlotte lives with a Ngāpuhi chief there.

*John Rutherford is an example of Pākehā-Māori.*

 PHOTOCOPYING OF THIS PAGE IS RESTRICTED UNDER LAW. 

James Caddell, about 16-years-old, works at night to club seals. One day he, with five others, lands on Stewart Island. Suddenly Māori attack. They kill the men, spare James. Does the chief's niece claim his life by throwing a cloak over him? Does James throw himself at the chief and beg for mercy which makes warriors step back because he touches the chief's mat and so becomes tapu? James marries the niece, adopts a Māori lifestyle, gets tattooed, becomes a warrior. He is lucky to be off that ship as its crew helps set off a Sealers' War of 1810-1821 – a series of fights between sealers and whalers on one side and Māori on the other.

John (Jacky) Guard is convicted of stealing a quilt, does years of hard labour in Sydney, sets up a whaling station in Tory Channel, marries 15-year-old Betty on a trip to Sydney, has a boy and a girl. He buys Kākāpō Bay from chiefs, moves his whaling station there. In 1834, his ship is driven ashore in Taranaki. Māori attack, loot, kill some crew, capture the rest and the Guards. Jacky is released to get gunpowder as ransom; at Sydney he gets Governor support for a rescue. A Sydney paper prints sensational reports of Māori savagery. A man-of-war and schooner go to Taranaki to rescue the captives. They bombard and burn pā. Accounts say they kill an elderly chief who carries the Guard boy on his back to the beach, and also the chief who protects Betty while Jacky is away. The Sydney paper prints further sensational stories. The British Parliament and other groups in England protest against violence towards Māori.

Kororāreka.

Trader Phillip Tapsell from Denmark says he worked, among other things, as a pirate, but now it is 1823 and he is marrying Maria Ringa in New Zealand. Less than a day later Maria runs away. He marries again. Karuhi, sister of a Ngāpuhi chief, who is fluent in English and will act as interpreter and guide. Te Arawa chiefs invite Tapsell to settle at Maketu as an agent of a Sydney trading outfit. He knows what Māori want and how clever they are at adapting. Give them nails and they can make chisels, hooks, fishhooks, drills, weapon tips. He knows Pākehā who say they are scared their vessels will sink if Māori get nails out of them. He surrounds his big house with 12 cannons. When Karuhi passes away, he marries Hine-i-tūrama Ngātiki, high-ranking Ngāti Whakaue of Te Arawa. She also helps him greatly in his trading activities through her chiefly connections. He is peacemaker in a war between Te Arawa and Ngāi Te Rangi at Maketu in 1833. But later a war party destroys Maketu pā. Tapsell watches his properties burn.

Two items of trade, muskets and mokomokai, damage relationships. Muskets set off an arms race among iwi and musket wars happen in both the North and South Islands in the early 19th century. Some historians say it is possible that more die in those wars than the 18,000 New Zealanders who die in World War 1. The wars set up new and complicated relationships among iwi and hapū. Some Māori are captured and used as slaves, some become refugees, some migrate to other places. Some iwi have their rohe changed, some areas are left with no people. There is unsettled utu, and there is not going to be a united Māori force of all iwi fighting a non-Māori force in the later New Zealand Wars. The musket wars end at the time British settlers want to buy land and the wars have muddled customary rights. It is easier for settlers to buy land without getting the okay from all iwi or hapū who may or may not now live on the land. Today some iwi argue that muskets led to unfair loss of land. Some ask for recognition of iwi boundaries that are there before muskets.

ISBN: 9780170462419 PHOTOCOPYING OF THIS PAGE IS RESTRICTED UNDER LAW. 

Back to Cook; when he visits Queen Charlotte Sound, a Māori paddles his waka out to the *Endeavour*. He has three mokomokai, dried human heads. Joseph Banks trades linen underwear for the head of a 14-year-old boy – another curio for him. People in Europe and America become interested in buying mokomokai to display in private collections, museums, medical institutions.

## Mahi Skills

1 **Local history:** Try to find out if there were early contacts between locals and Europeans in your area.

2 **Understanding changing attitudes:** Today New Zealand works to bring mokomokai home. They lie in special wāhi tapu at Te Papa. So sacred that few people are allowed to see them. Explain what an attitude is, and suggest reasons for changing attitudes to mokomokai.

3 **Understanding criticism:** This painting shows an 1809 event that causes the deaths of sailors and Māori and which some people say delays the British Government making New Zealand a colony. Find out about the event and a central figure in it called Te Pahi, and why the painting is today criticised as being romantic or having a political agenda.

*The Boyd exploding.*

4 **Understanding links with British Government:** Londoner Samuel Polack comes to New Zealand in 1831 and does well as a trader. From a wealthy family, he knows how the British Empire operates. Back in England for a visit he gives evidence to the House of Lords about how unorganised European settlement is not good for Māori, how Māori will survive only through organised colonisation, how Māori will welcome colonisation, how colonisation will benefit Māori minds and bodies through employment by 'civilised persons'. Imagine Polack takes a Māori chief with him to the House of Lords. Now imagine what the chief might say and make some notes about it.

5 **Origin of a word:** Time now to look at the word Pākehā because not all non-Māori arriving are from Europe. Find out where the word might come from.


PHOTOCOPYING OF THIS PAGE IS RESTRICTED UNDER LAW.
ISBN: 9780170462419

# Missionary Interaction

7

**Historians talk about interaction. By that they mean how groups of people get along with each other once a relationship is set up. Another group who interact with Māori is missionaries – people who go to places to spread their religion. Mission stations have churches, houses, farms, gardens, and schools to teach religion, reading and writing, and English to Māori. Many missionaries see colonisation and British government as good for Māori.**

Samuel Marsden is a priest of the Anglican Church of England in the British colony of New South Wales. I want to set up a mission station in New Zealand, he decides. One day in Sydney he meets Ngāpuhi chief Ruatara who is crewing on a whaler. Ruatara and hundreds of kin live in a pā and kāinga above Rangihoua Bay in Northland. On 22 December 1814, Marsden's ship anchors below Ruatara's kāinga. He has brought three missionary families, and chiefs Ruatara, Hongi Hika and Korokoro who have been in Sydney, and a group of men to build a mission station. The local people weep over their returning chiefs. Next day they get the livestock off the ship. A cow causes chaos by running among people. Marsden causes astonishment by riding a horse along the beach. Next day there is a formal welcome to the missionary ship. Hundreds of Māori, some Pākehā, a fleet of waka. The ship's captain fires gun salutes. Warriors, including some females, line up on the beach and put on a mock battle. On Christmas Day Samuel Marsden stands on an upturned canoe hull and preaches in English. Ruatara translates. Ruatara is now the protector of his Pākehā.

*Samuel Marsden preaches while Ruatara, beside him, and Korokoro, foreground left, wear British uniforms from the NSW Governor.*

ISBN: 9780170462419
PHOTOCOPYING OF THIS PAGE IS RESTRICTED UNDER LAW.

*Missionaries William and Henry Williams try to stop a taua.*

Missionaries begin to clear the terraced site at Hohi, a small bay below the pā, for the mission station. Some historians say it is Mission Impossible. The site is small, steep, has poor soil and not much sun, is open to waka raids. Life for missionaries is tough while they wait for houses to go up. Shelters are flimsy and flood water pours through. They have to cook outside, and have only hand tools, barrows and baskets. They depend on Māori to trade for food such as pork and potatoes while they wait for a ship to bring provisions from Sydney. No timber for buildings so they have to barter and bring it in on rafts behind their rowboats. The beach is the site for killing of captives and ritual feasting. Gradually buildings go up at Rangihoua and missionaries learn te reo Māori. But arguments sometimes lead to fist fights among missionaries. There are scandals – adultery, drunkenness, affairs. After one missionary is accused of misconduct, the others burn his gear and shoot his horse. When a missionary is sacked, his Māori supporters come for muru against his home and schoolhouse. They break windows and doors, pull off weatherboards.

To start with, Māori see missionaries as another group of Pākehā with which to trade. They interact but keep their own beliefs and customs. A rangatira drinks from a mission cup and to prevent breaches of tapu breaks the cup or takes it away. A Pākehā disturbs a wāhi tapu and touches bones, so a tohunga removes tapu by smashing dishes and kitchen tools the Pākehā uses. And soon Māori give missionaries a real headache. We will trade for muskets, they say. We are not allowed to trade in muskets, missionaries insist.

When Ruatara gets sick with a fever and dies, senior Ngāpuhi chief and uncle Hongi Hika takes over as patron. He is also patron to other missions set up at Kerikeri and Waimate North.


PHOTOCOPYING OF THIS PAGE IS RESTRICTED UNDER LAW.
ISBN: 9780170462419

In August 1823 a new Mission leader, the Reverend Henry Williams, arrives to start a new mission settlement at Paihia. He learns te reo Māori. A printing press with books in te reo Māori help Māori learn to read and write. Williams, trying to keep the peace, follows Ngāpuhi taua south. He becomes a trusted peacemaker during iwi wars.

## Mahi Skills

1 **Local history:** Think location and describe why interaction with missionaries will be different in the Bay of Islands to inland areas.

2 **Sketching to establish meaning:** Make simple sketches to show the following: *mission station, pā and kāinga, colony of New South Wales.*

3 **Referencing:** Work out to whom the following refer and why.

a Te Waharoa of Waikato entrusts him with his patu to deliver to Ngāpuhi rangatira Tāreha as a peace token.

b Port Jackson people warn him missionaries will bring settlers and soldiers who will take land and reduce Māori to the bad condition of Australian Aborigines but Marsden reassures him by offering to turn back the missionary ship.

c Some of them give in and begin trading in muskets.

d Has a reputation as the flogging parson in Australia although research suggests he may sentence convicts to flogging less often and less harshly than other NSW magistrates.

e Ex-navy man who fights in the Napoleonic wars before becoming an Anglican priest and who, at Paihia, oversees the building and launching of missionary schooner *Herald* which only a few years later is wrecked on the Hokianga bar.

4 **Being logical:** Write out the following and add the missing words from the list below.

The first high-ranking ... to become ... is Ngāpuhi Rāwiri Taiwhanga who has been one of Hongi Hika's ... Tattooed, he is ... at Paihia 1830. He starts work at the Kerikeri ... station as a foreman and gets paid an ... a month. A quick learner, he becomes an excellent gardener and farmer. On his own ... he makes butter for sale – so he is called the first ... dairy farmer in New Zealand. He ... European clothing and teaches his children European ways.

**Missing words:**

| | | |
|---|---|---|
| baptised | adopts | farm |
| commercial | warriors | axe |
| mission | Christian | Māori |

5 **Expanding:** Historians say Ruatara shows Māori do not sit back and let Pākehā contact swamp them. Suggest facts that seem to back it up.

ISBN: 9780170462419
PHOTOCOPYING OF THIS PAGE IS RESTRICTED UNDER LAW.

# 8 Letter to a Sovereign

**Historians use documents to find out and show what people at the time think and do. They know these primary sources can be reliable witnesses and add a human face to an event.**

It is early October 1831. Thirteen Ngāpuhi rangatira are having a hui at Kororipo pā in Kerikeri about writing a letter to British King William IV. Hongi Hika's visit to England has already set up a relationship with the monarchy there. Rangatira to rangatira. Hongi, and chief Waikato, meet the King and records suggest they all have a good time. The King is trying to divorce his wife and Hongi is said to say *his* wives cause him no trouble. The King gives the chiefs a tour of his palace and presents muskets, a coat of chain mail and a helmet.

The pā's history is closely linked to Hongi Hika who dies in 1828. It is a key place from which he looks after his affairs at Kerikeri and launches taua. Phillip Tapsell, on a whaling ship, records waka landing 40 prisoners who are put in a row and tomahawked. After the return of one taua, the pā and waters around it are made tapu due to the burial there of fallen chiefs. Missionaries break tapu by towing logs in. Chief Wairua threatens violence but receives an axe as utu.

Today the chiefs talk about the tribe of Marion. He is the French explorer Marion du Fresne who visits the Bay of Islands in 1772 and is killed by locals with 24 of his crew. The French then kill an estimated 250 Māori, burn pā and kāinga, and destroy waka.

In the earlier musket wars, Hongi and allies set out with muskets in waka taua against enemy iwi in the south and waka return decorated with severed heads. And males are not the only ones with respected history here. Turikatuku, said to be Hongi Hika's favourite wife and most trusted adviser even though she goes blind, tells Ngāpuhi at a famous battle of the musket wars, Be brave. Remember your return to wives and children depends on this. Defeat will mean being killed and eaten or wretched slavery for life. Turikatuku and Hongi's son is killed; Ngāpuhi kill hundreds of Ngāti Whātua and chase survivors into Waikato.

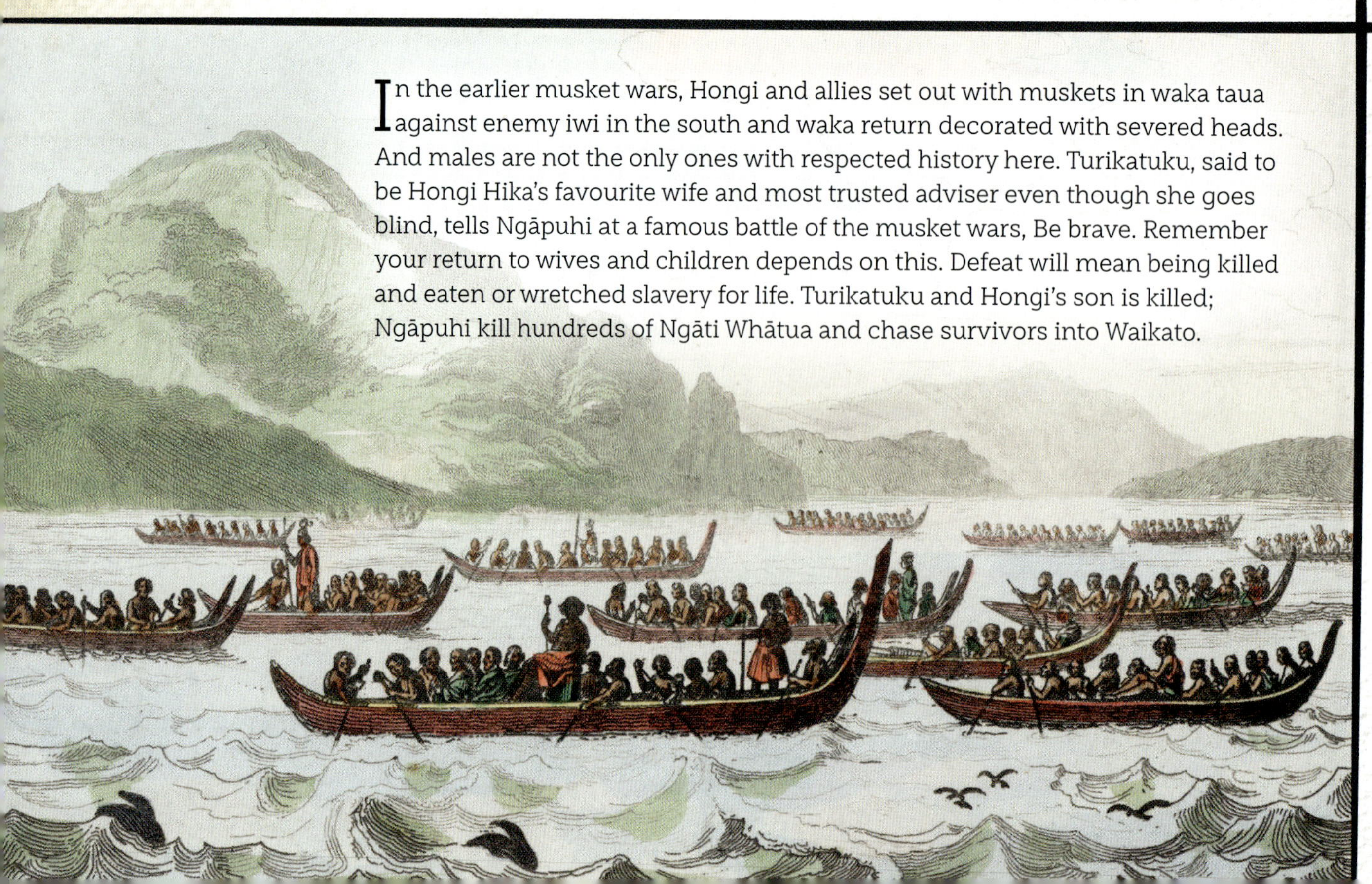

Last month Rewa, who is Hongi Hika's successor and is at this Kororipo hui, comes back from Sydney with news that a French naval vessel is on its way. Missionary wife Marianne Williams records in her diary that a Māori runs to tell her the ship has come, that it has 400 enemies of King William come to spy out the land, that she must give him a flag to hoist. The ship is not a warship but rumours swirl that the tribe of Marion is planning to settle in New Zealand.

Who organises this hui? Missionary Williams notes that on 28 September several chiefs come to discuss a letter from rangatira to the British monarch and at a hui at Kerikeri on 4 October the wording of the letter is settled. The original letter is written in Māori. A missionary is thought to have translated it into English. Then there is Eruera Pare Hongi – Edward Parry, educated at the Kerikeri mission school and perhaps a nephew of Hongi Hika. Some say he drafts and writes the letter. The letter is called a petition because it is a formal written and signed request asking for help from someone with authority. It is addressed To King William, The Gracious Chief of England. It says the chiefs have heard the tribe of Marion is coming to take their land. They ask the king to become friend and guardian. Best that he deals with British people behaving badly such as interfering with Māori ways and running away from the king's trading ships, because otherwise the misbehaving ones will experience Māori anger. The letter is shipped off.

*Eruera Pare Hongi.*

## Mahi Skills

1 **Local history:** Some iwi say events up north are Ngāpuhi affairs. But events such as the letter impact on other iwi, and on Pākehā. Explain how that might happen.

2 **Having a smile at history:** Moehanga (Te Mahanga) of Ngāpuhi is the first recorded Māori to visit England, on 27 April 1806. In 2021, social media in New Zealand celebrate Moehanga Day – the day Māori discover Britain. Describe the relationship between the factual visit and the fictional national day.

3 **British etiquette:** Until this time the British Parliament does not take much notice of events in New Zealand. British etiquette – the polite way of behaving and code of conduct – will now come into play. Suggest what might happen next.

4 **General and specific:** New Zealand is now known to other countries, not just Britain. Suggest general reasons the letter is written to start with, and then specific reasons why it is written to King William IV.

5 **Looking at action:** Name a person to whom one of these actions belongs. *Breaks tapu. Gets balance restored by a gift. Reigns in a country. Attends a meeting. Writes about an event.*

# 9 A British Resident

**Historians know history is about causes and results. They try not to leave loose ends. They want to show what happens next. Such as the result of the letter to the king.**

A reply to the letter comes next year in the form of James Busby. He is a Scotsman and an expert in viticulture (wine-making). He has never been to New Zealand but presents ideas about it to the Colonial Office. A Resident with the authority of a magistrate, he says, should be sent to protect the British by delivering up runaway convicts, and working with missionaries to persuade Māori 'to abandon the ferocious character of the savage and the cannibal'. He puts himself forward for the job, sends bottles of wine to the Secretary and gets the job.

*James Busby.*

On 17 May 1833, a ship brings Busby to the Bay of Islands. Sailors row him ashore at Paihia where about 50 Pākehā wait, and about 600 Māori do a haka. In the church, missionary Williams asks for the great seal on the royal letter to be broken and Busby reads the letter aloud. It says the King has sent Busby to stay among Māori as the King's man, to be called British Resident, to be a mediator between Māori and the King's people living with them. Williams translates into Māori this letter and Busby's following speech. Some chiefs reply. Busby should have brought soldiers to protect him, says one. A rumour says missionaries and the Resident will get paid for Māori who turn Christian, says another. Busby presents blankets and tobacco to the chiefs. Pākehā go to eat beef and potatoes at the Mission House and Māori to also eat stirabout.

*Mission station at Paihia, 1827.*

Busby may not yet realise his chances of success are low. He is to rescue Māori from evils Pākehā have exposed them to, yet he will not get on well with some missionaries. He is to encourage Māori towards a form of government yet iwi and hapū have their own rangatira. He is to protect 'well disposed settlers and traders', prevent 'outrages' by Pākehā against Māori, catch criminals and escaped convicts and return them, yet he has no soldiers, no police, no authority to arrest, and little money. He is to ask for help from the Governor in Australia, yet he is on bad terms with him and the Governor does not think much of him, will hardly ever consult him and is not keen to spend money or time on New Zealand. No wonder Busby rarely goes far from the Bay. No wonder Māori call him the man-of-war without guns.


PHOTOCOPYING OF THIS PAGE IS RESTRICTED UNDER LAW.
ISBN: 9780170462419

Busby's house today.

Busby's pre-cut house frame shipped from Sydney goes up at Waitangi under the protection of Ngāti Rāhiri rangatira Te Kēmara. Māori can use their settlements and whare there when they come for fishing trips. On 30 April 1834 Busby's servant wakes him. Māori have broken in, he says. Busby and the servant rush out, get shot at, retreat and fire their own guns. Splinters from a musket ball that hits a doorpost injure Busby's face. Mrs Busby has given birth two days earlier. The intruders take items from the servant's bedroom. Busby sends a message to Williams at Paihia. Boats from several ships land below the house. Sailors armed with muskets, pistols, lances, and harpoons storm around but the intruders have gone. Next day Māori gather at Waitangi and say it was not them. A hui of chiefs fails to come up with a plan. Several months later the wife of a local chief finds the servant's rug in her home. The chief is brought before his fellow chiefs and confesses. The chiefs decide he must give up land and be banished. Almost a year later there is another hui for chiefs to decide how to carry out the sentence. After news that Busby will give blankets to those who go with him, some chiefs and Busby go to a kāinga where the chief sees them coming and leaves. Busby asks the chief's relations to burn down his huts. Chiefs share out his possessions. They do not make the chief leave the area. Busby's ideas of law and justice are based on individual responsibilities and rights. Māori ideas are based on utu and balance in relationships. The Governor still refuses to send a warship or soldiers to Busby.

## Mahi Skills

1 **Local history:** A photo library has an image of the church at Paihia with this incorrect caption: *The church, where after landing in 1881, James Busby signed an accord between British Government and thirteen Maori Chiefs. Eight years prior to the Treaty of Waitangi.* Find an image of the church and write a correct caption.

2 **Avoiding assumptions:** Assumption is something you accept as true without asking for proof. Accounts at this time mention hosts giving Māori guests stirabout – a mixture of boiled flour and water and maybe sugar, while Pākehā get meat and potatoes. Some people assume Māori are being disrespected. But some others say stirabout is a treat and some Māori ask for it in exchange for produce. Use stirabout to show how assumptions can cause misunderstanding. You might think about why Māori, who have had to try to get rid of fibre in aruhe (fern root), welcome stirabout.

3 **Understanding legends:** The land Busby's house is on has a long human history. Find the legend about Maikuku and the tangi (wailing) of a taniwha.

4 **Applying a saying:** There is an English saying of 'being on a hiding to nothing'. Check you know its meaning and then apply it to James Busby.

5 **Using text:** Write out some sentences to show increasing contact between rangatiratanga and sovereignty.

# 10 Flag and Declaration

**Historians know the historical record may sometimes be a mix of facts and theory. It is a fact that New Zealand gets a flag in 1834. There are theories for why it gets the flag. Historians also look at reactions and chain reactions – how one event leads to another and that leads to another. All the reactions from the beginning of this book onwards have been leading towards the possibility of war. Now the reactions are speeding up because colonisation is about to begin.**

*Flag of the United Tribes of New Zealand.*

Flags are part of British culture. The Union Jack shows people are united under one government and one monarch. In the 1830s a decision is made to get New Zealand a flag. Some historians say it is because when a trading ship built in Hokianga is in Sydney in 1830 with a cargo of timber and flax, and maybe one or more rangatira taking the chance to visit New South Wales are on board, customs seize the ship as it is unregistered with no national flag. Other historians poke holes in this. New Zealand ships, they say, are not at this stage liable for seizure if they have no national flag. Another theory is that Busby thinks a flag will help chiefs work together in the style of British government he wants. But he needs a reason for getting iwi to be more united.

Busby writes to New South Wales and suggests a New Zealand flag be created. He submits drawings of three flags prepared by Williams and says they are to be shown to chiefs. The Governor gets the designs sewn up into flags and a warship brings them to Busby at Waitangi. Busby invites leading rangatira to meet at Waitangi on 20 March 1834. Twenty-five chiefs from the north arrive. So do settlers, missionaries and naval officers. Each chief votes for a design. The winning flag is the one on the missionary ship. Busby declares it is now the national flag and has it hoisted. The warship gives a gun salute. Busby invites Pākehā to a meal at his house. Māori get stirabout. The new flag is sent back to New South Wales, then to King William IV who approves it. It becomes known as Te Kara o Te Whakaminenga o Ngā Hapū o Nu Tīreni – the Flag of the United Tribes of New Zealand.

One day in 1835 Busby is opening his mail. What's this? A letter from that Frenchman de Thierry? He wants to set up a colony in Hokianga with himself as Governor? Claims chiefs sold him 40,000 acres? He's in Tahiti waiting for an armed ship to bring him here? Busby reacts. He sends a letter to de Thierry. He uses the words mischief, madness, criminality and tells him if he turns up he will meet with spirited resistance from the whole population. He sends a letter to New South Wales saying he wants to call a meeting of chiefs so they can declare the independence of New Zealand. He prints a circular for settlers warning de Thierry might get 'influence over the simple-minded Natives'. He drafts a Declaration of the Independence of New Zealand. He sends the draft to Henry Williams. Will


PHOTOCOPYING OF THIS PAGE IS RESTRICTED UNDER LAW.
ISBN: 9780170462419

you translate this into Māori? he asks. He sends an invitation to local rangatira to meet at his house on 28 October. This is what Busby says happened, that the Declaration is down to him and Williams. But some people say Māori, at least Edward Parry, have input into it.

Busby gives rangatira who come to the hui a blanket and pork. They debate the declaration and 34 sign it. This Whakaputanga o te Rangatiratanga o Nu Tīreni (Declaration of Independence of the United Tribes of New Zealand) says Te Whakaminenga o Ngā Hapū o Nu Tīreni – the United Tribes of New Zealand, have kīngitanga (sovereign power) and mana (authority), no foreigners can make laws, tribes will meet at Waitangi each autumn to make laws, they ask for King William's protection against threats to their mana in return for them protecting British people, they thank the King for acknowledging their flag.

Busby sends it to the New South Wales Government and the Colonial Office and it goes on to King William IV. One official says it is silly. One says it has good things in it. In May 1836 the British Government acknowledges getting an English translation of it. By July 1839 another 18 chiefs have signed. It is published in Māori newspapers, read aloud at Māori gatherings. Does it have the idea of a Māori sense of identity and the idea of New Zealand as a state? Does it show iwi and hapū have their own mana but can work together on common interests? Will it help Māori cope with challenges brought by Europeans? Or is it a step towards making New Zealand a British colony?

*Baron de Thierry.*

Many groups and individuals tell the British Government it should make New Zealand a colony. It is not sure. Colonies can behave like naughty children and run away from the Mother Country. Keeping British soldiers and officials in colonies is very expensive. But maybe it should encourage Māori to amalgamate with settler society, to make a good future with settlers. It needs legal authority to deal with British settlers in New Zealand, and to stop other countries claiming it. Because Britain has recognised the Declaration of Independence, it will need to have a formal arrangement. Rangatira signed the Declaration and so it will have to be with them.

*Voting for the flag; the artist has made mistakes such as Busby looking too old.*

When de Thierry arrives in 1837, chiefs deny his claim to the 40,000 acres and offer him 800 acres on condition he gives up the larger claim. He does but his settlers riot and take off.

Into the mix now comes another group – the New Zealand Company. Englishman Edward Gibbon Wakefield is the brains behind it. Often in trouble at school and then in 1816 he elopes with a 16-year-old heiress. She dies and he abducts a 15-year-old heiress who he has never met before. He flees to France and agents of the girl's parents capture him. He is put on trial in England and gets three years in prison. There he has time to flesh out his ideas about colonisation. He plans to colonise New Zealand. The New Zealand Company sends a ship off to New Zealand in 1839 to set things up for British settlers. In charge of this expedition is William, one of Edward's brothers. The ship goes to Port Nicholson (Wellington Harbour). William buys a huge amount of land from Māori.

Edward sells the idea of living in New Zealand to people in Britain. A paradise on earth, he says. Excellent for British settlers. Māori are keen to welcome you. By the end of 1839 British people are boarding Company ships and sailing off to New Zealand.

*Edward Gibbon Wakefield.*

Time then for the British Government to decide what to do. Māori have no input because they are not at the British Parliament in London; they are thousands of miles away. One Māori is believed to be even further south. Tuati, whose mother is Ngāpuhi and father the whaler and sealer after whom Stewart Island is named, is with an expedition finding evidence that Antarctica is a continent. Today it has a peak called Tuati. Between his trip to America to join the expedition and his leaving the expedition, his country becomes a British colony.

## Mahi Skills

1 **Local history:** Explain why knowledge of Tuati will be housed in New Zealand, such as with whānau, rather than Antarctica.

2 **Detecting changing attitudes:** The Whakaputanga o te Rangatiratanga o Nu Tīreni document is gnawed by rats, and one time almost goes up in smoke. Today it lives in the He Tohu exhibition at the National Library. Comment on a changed attitude towards preserving history.

3 **Listing:** List ideas about British government and organisation from this chapter.

4 **Economic decisions:** Prepare a short piece in any format to show how by 1830 British economic matters are appearing in New Zealand.

5 **New input:** At hearings in Northland, about 170 years into the future, Māori will say that even earlier than He Whakaputanga, Māori in the north met to talk about issues such as how best to deal with incoming Europeans, that their ancestors had input into the drafting of He Whakaputanga, that even though Busby never convened the congress of chiefs after 1835, Ngāpuhi histories show that Te Whakaminenga kept meeting. Comment on how new ways of thinking about reactions to actions may arrive at any time.


PHOTOCOPYING OF THIS PAGE IS RESTRICTED UNDER LAW.
ISBN: 9780170462419

# Treaty 11

**Historians have been writing about, talking about and debating the Treaty of Waitangi since 1840. They know that the details of the days before the signing are important to show how and why it exists.**

The British decide. They send off a man called William Hobson. A British naval officer who signed up as a 10-year-old. He is often sick with yellow fever he picked up chasing pirates in the West Indies. He is considered to have honour and courage. The British give him instructions. (Aborigines is a term used for indigenous people so here it means Māori.) He is to '... treat with the Aborigines ... for the recognition of Her Majesty's sovereign authority over the whole or any parts of those islands which they may be willing to place under Her Majesty's dominion .... All dealings with the Aborigines for their Lands must be conducted on the same principles of sincerity, justice and good faith ...'

*William Hobson.*

Hobson leaves London and arrives at Sydney on 14 December 1839. The Governor tells him he will be British Consul and Lieutenant-Governor. He gives him four police troopers, a sergeant, civil servants, treasurer, Surveyor-General, Chief Clerk, Police Magistrate, to serve in his colonial administration. He arrives in New Zealand on 29 January. He is sick. He and Joseph Nias, the captain of the ship bringing Hobson to New Zealand, have had loud arguments. In the morning the ship anchors off Kororāreka. Busby arrives and boards. Hobson gives him a letter from the British Government telling him he has lost his job. Busby copes. He helps Hobson get invites out to Europeans at Kororāreka to gather next day to hear Hobson read out his official documents, and invites to the confederated chiefs to meet Hobson at Busby's place the following Wednesday, 5 February 1840.

Signing the Treaty.

On 30 January Hobson goes to the church at Kororāreka. British officials expect him to land as British Consul and later call himself Lieutenant-Governor of any lands he gets. But Hobson says he is Lieutenant-Governor from the start. Busby disapproves. Captain Nias disapproves, so strongly he refuses to fire a 13-gun salute marking Hobson's arrival. He fires the 11-gun salute for a consul. About 300 settlers and 100 Māori listen to Hobson. My duties as Lieutenant-Governor of New Zealand have started, he says. From now on, private land-buying from Māori will be null and void. And apparently someone has told Māori he plans to make them slaves of Queen Victoria.

Now Hobson, who has no legal training, has to write a treaty. There is no evidence of rangatira having input. No evidence that Hobson has a draft to work from. Hobson does not understand te reo Māori and not all Māori understand English. It seems he dictates a draft to his clerk on board. He is too sick to leave the ship so the clerk and treasurer take the draft to Busby, who revises the draft.

On 4 February the ship's officers and sailors bring spars and sails and make a big tent in front of Busby's house. About 4 pm Hobson brings the draft treaty in English to missionary Henry Williams to translate. Williams' 21-year-old son Edward is a fluent speaker of northern Māori so he helps Henry work on the treaty translation that night. There is no evidence that Māori help with this translation. On 5 February at 9 am Hobson and Captain Nias arrive at Busby's House. Busby, Hobson, and Henry Williams work on the final draft of the treaty. Waka, boats and ships come from all directions. Stalls sell food and drink – pork, bread, pies, biscuits, cold roasts, ham, ale, spirits.

About 500 Māori and 200 Pākehā gather. In the tent male and female Māori rangatira sit in a semicircle, some with dogskin mats, others in blankets or cloaks. Bishop Jean-Baptiste Pompallier arrives wearing his purple gown and stockings, big ruby ring, gold chain and crucifix. He goes into Busby's house. Anglican missionaries in their plain black dress notice his boldness. About 11 am Hobson and Nias walk behind troopers to the tent. At the table Henry Williams sits on Hobson's right, beside Captain Nias. Pompallier and priest on the left. Anglican missionaries have to stand behind Williams. The number in the tent is estimated at 400, about half Māori and half Pākehā.

Tikanga says locals open speeches. But the visitors take charge. Hobson addresses chiefs in English. Henry Williams translates. Hobson says, The Queen has sent me here as Governor and she asks you to sign this treaty and so give her power to restrain her people here who break the laws. Williams reads out the treaty in Māori. It is short with only three articles. He explains it, says missionaries approve it, it is an act of love from the Queen who wants to secure to Māori their property, rights and privileges, and is a fortress against any foreign power. Busby stands and speaks. Hobson has come to assure you of possession of your lands, he says. Land not properly bought by Europeans will be returned. Then rangatira speak. Henry Williams translates their speeches into English. Some are for the treaty and some are against. Hobson announces the gathering will reconvene on Friday, 7 February. Māori are given tobacco. The crowd does three cheers and breaks up.


PHOTOCOPYING OF THIS PAGE IS RESTRICTED UNDER LAW.
ISBN: 9780170462419

That night many rangatira camp on the Paihia side of Waitangi River at Te Rou Rangatira, where Te Tii marae is now. They debate whether to sign the treaty. Williams and other missionaries are with them. Williams says they went through the treaty showing the advantages of Māori being taken under the fostering care of the British Government.

It is now 6 February and food is running out. Missionaries realise some rangatira are about to go. They send a message to Hobson to come and collect signatures. He arrives in civilian dress instead of naval uniform except for his hat. No more speeches, he says. Only signatures. Will you guarantee religious freedom? Pompallier asks. Hobson agrees and it is recorded. Although this does not appear on the Treaty, some people say it is part of it and call it the fourth article.

Henry Williams begins to call out names. Finally Hōne Heke signs. Others follow. Today, Māori say that rangatira who used nose tattoo as signatures make the document tapu. Hobson gives each rangatira blankets, tobacco and potatoes. Patuone presents a greenstone mere to Hobson for Queen Victoria. Hobson invites him to dinner on his ship.

## Mahi Skills

1 **Local history:** Between February and September missionaries, traders and officials take Treaty copies around the country for rangatira to sign. State how that sets up local histories with the Treaty.

2 **Translating:** When rangatira sign, Hobson says, He iwi tahi tātou. It is usually translated as *We are one people*. But some say a more accurate translation is *Together we are one nation*. Explain the difference.

3 **Oration:** Rangatira are skilled in oration. One account says Tāreha of Ngāti Rēhia, a big man with a deep voice and who is dressed in matting, speaks. Do you think we are poor and needy and poverty-stricken, he says, that we really need your foreign garments, your food? (He holds up a bundle of fern-roots.) If all were to be alike, all equal in rank with you – but you, the Governor up high (he holds up a paddle) and I down, under, beneath! No, no, no. Describe how he uses props.

4 **Recognising tone:** Tone is the general feeling or mood of something such as a letter. Read this invite to rangatira from Busby and comment on its tone. Respectful? Rude?

> My dear friend, I make contact with you again. A warship has arrived with a chief on board sent by the Queen of England to be a Governor for us both. Now he suggests that all the chiefs of the Confederation of New Zealand, on Wednesday of this holy week coming should gather to meet him. So I ask you my friend to come to this meeting here at Waitangi, at my home. You are a chief of that Confederation. And so, to conclude.
> From your dear friend, Busby.

5 **Conventions:** Conventions are the way things are usually done. List as many British conventions from this chapter as you can. The first might be very young boys joining the Navy. At this time the conventional thought is that sailors are best trained when young.

 PHOTOCOPYING OF THIS PAGE IS RESTRICTED UNDER LAW. 

# 12 Colonisation

**Historians look at how groups make and use rules and laws and how the rules and laws affect individuals and communities. Colonisation is how the British make and use rules to get control of lands they take over. It can lead to conflict.**

The Treaty is copied by hand and printing press so people on foot, horses, boats and ships can take copies around for iwi to sign. About another 500 Māori put names or moko on it. All but 39 sign the Māori text. Pākehā assume signatures are male. Yet some Māori females are important leaders and rangatira and at least 13 sign.

Why rangatira sign varies from place to place. Generally, reasons may include the idea that Māori outnumber settlers and so will keep control of their own affairs, that they have a personal relationship with the British monarch, that manuhiri will respect tikanga, that the Governor will protect chiefly mana, that missionaries say the Treaty will be good for Māori, that the French might come, that it is too late to stop contact, that they will get technologies and goods, that settlement will be controlled, that the Governor will control land-buyers and trespassers on Māori land breaking tapu, that settlers will want more Māori labour to provide services such as building, that trade for Māori produce will increase.

The two parties who sign the Treaty, Māori and Crown, have different understandings of it. Experts say Māori and English texts do not always match up. The English text suggests Māori give the Crown absolutely all rights and powers of sovereignty – supreme power and government – whereas the Māori text has Māori giving kāwanatanga katoa – complete governorship. For many, kāwanatanga suggests Māori keep their own authority to manage their own affairs and give the right of governorship to the Queen in return for protection. Māori are guaranteed tino rangatiratanga, control of land, property, taonga.

One action the British Empire does is colonise. Its people settle among indigenous people of another land and establish control through actions such as bringing in British laws. The action is called colonisation. The place colonised is a colony. Britain's Colonial Office in London sends a man called a Governor to live in the colony and run it. Two dates are important for the beginning of New Zealand's colonisation. On 21 May 1840 Hobson proclaims sovereignty (supreme power and authority) over all New Zealand. For almost a year New Zealand is part of the New South Wales colony. On 3 May 1841 Hobson becomes Governor and Commander-in-Chief of New Zealand and New Zealand becomes a colony separate from New South Wales.

*The Waitangi Sheet of the Treaty of Waitangi.*


PHOTOCOPYING OF THIS PAGE IS RESTRICTED UNDER LAW.
ISBN: 9780170462419

*The British Empire.*

For a while British officials try to take tikanga into account while bringing in British laws. Two laws let Māori convicted of theft pay money to the victim in compensation – a form of muru. Another law says legal disputes involving Māori are to be heard by a magistrate with two Māori chiefs.

Sometimes laws backfire. Hobson bans cutting down kauri to stop dishonest people taking trees. But to Māori it is Government interfering in a Ngāpuhi source of income. Sometimes soldiers and police magistrates arrest Māori and an appeal to the Treaty of Waitangi is made. Defence for one Māori accused of taking a blanket from a settler argues the Treaty gives the right of getting justice for iwi members to rangatira. The Crown says getting justice is not a traditional job of a chief and this is not an iwi matter because a settler is involved. For many places, Māori have had little or no contact with the British and nothing much changes for a while. Iwi and hapū continue to be in charge. When some Ngāi Te Rangi attack some Te Arawa sailing in Tauranga harbour, troops from Auckland arrive, Bishop Selwyn arrives, the Chief Justice arrives, and Māori sort it out themselves without further bloodshed.

Generally though, British officials tend to think of Māori being under British rule, regardless of whether their rangatira signed the Treaty or not. So do settlers and after 1840 there are thousands of them. Two events of 1841–42 suggest to Māori that British law is being favoured. The first involves Motuarohia Island that John Roberton buys from Ngāpuhi chiefs to farm. The official story says John drowns, and leaves a widow Elizabeth and a young boy and girl. Settler Thomas Bull, who has been in trouble for robbing a ship, works on the farm. He hires Maketū Wharetōtara, who is 16 or 17 and the son of a Ngāpuhi chief.

Three-year-old Isabella Brind is placed in Elizabeth's care. The official story is that one day in November 1841 Maketū reacts to someone abusing him and damaging his mana. He kills Bull, Elizabeth, son and daughter, and Isabella. He burns the house and goes to his village in a waka. Authorities arrest three settlers but Maketū is said to have confessed. About 20 chiefs meet and most agree British justice should operate. Authorities send Maketū to Auckland for trial. He pleads not guilty but is sentenced and hanged on 7 March 1842. Some believe Maketū is innocent. They say Bull is the killer and Maketū, using utu, kills Bull. For years afterwards whenever the Chief Justice responsible for Maketū's sentence visits kāinga or pā he is introduced as having condemned Maketū to death. There are rumours that utu means the Governor will be killed.

*Maketū.*

Within a year, someone murders Rangihoua Kuika, daughter of a chief, with her baby son near Nelson. The suspect is Richard Cook, whaler and escaped convict. A missionary persuades Māori to let Crown justice deal with it. The case collapses. Cook is freed. He is said to confess before he leaves the area. Over a hundred years later at a hearing, Ngāti Toa will say evidence could easily have been got from other witnesses and this event made their people angry and upset with British justice.

## Mahi Skills

1 **Local history:** Explain what the word whanaunga means in the following sentence.

*Picture the huge crowds on Auckland's Queen Street at noon 7 March 1842 witnessing the execution of Maketū, and how his whanaunga will never forget.*

2 **Highlighting government:** Give reasons Māori may have had for signing the Treaty and highlight ones to do with government and organisation.

3 **Understanding concepts:** Concepts are general ideas. Explain the following: *colonisation, colony, empire, Crown, manuhiri, marae, justice, kawanatanga, sovereignty, tino rangatiratanga.*

4 **Diagram:** Make a diagram to show this concept. Māori rangatira for each hapū and iwi = Many different sources of power. British monarch and Parliament for all = One source of power.

5 **Oblique aerial:** Motuarohia (Roberton) Island. This is an oblique aerial photo as it is taken at an angle. Make a sketch of it to show the natural features.

PHOTOCOPYING OF THIS PAGE IS RESTRICTED UNDER LAW. ISBN: 9780170462419

# European Immigration

13

**Historians understand cause-and-effect relationships where one action or event (cause) leads to another action or event (effect). They show a cause-and-effect relationship with European settlement helping sovereignty bang into rangatiratanga.**

In Britain an Industrial Revolution creates cities with factories, slums, disease, pollution, bad working and living conditions. It makes many workers board ships for New Zealand. Others have different reasons. An ex-smuggler wants to reform himself. A wealthy man wants to be an artist but his father wants him in the church. A man introduces a fiancée to his father and father runs off with fiancée. The wife of a circus worker is killed by a horse and the worker is desperate to find a place where there is no chance of seeing a circus tent.

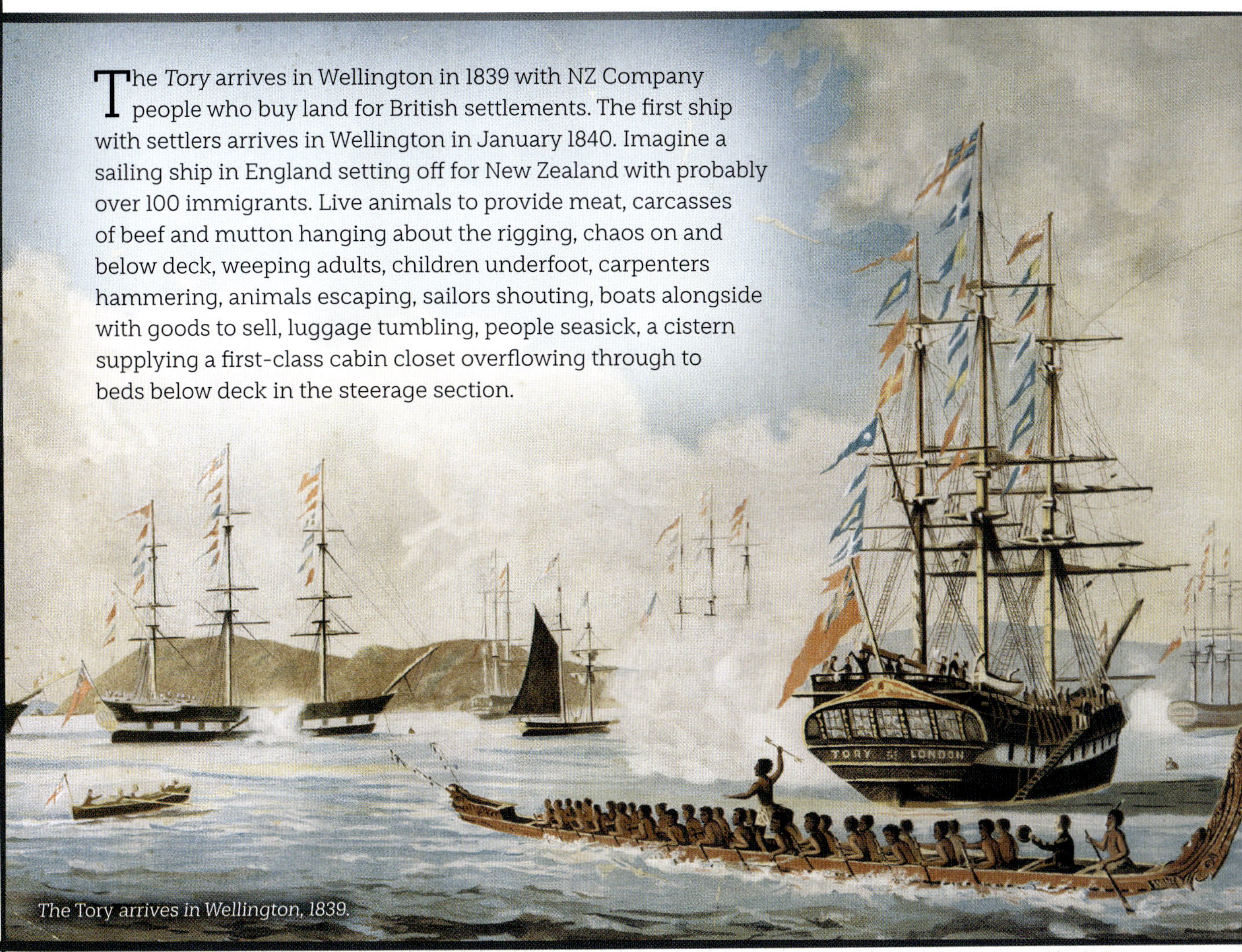


The *Tory* arrives in Wellington in 1839 with NZ Company people who buy land for British settlements. The first ship with settlers arrives in Wellington in January 1840. Imagine a sailing ship in England setting off for New Zealand with probably over 100 immigrants. Live animals to provide meat, carcasses of beef and mutton hanging about the rigging, chaos on and below deck, weeping adults, children underfoot, carpenters hammering, animals escaping, sailors shouting, boats alongside with goods to sell, luggage tumbling, people seasick, a cistern supplying a first-class cabin closet overflowing through to beds below deck in the steerage section.

*The Tory arrives in Wellington, 1839.*

ISBN: 9780170462419
PHOTOCOPYING OF THIS PAGE IS RESTRICTED UNDER LAW.

The ship at the mercy of winds and roaring seas, water sweeping over decks, timbers groaning as if the vessel is going to break into bits, a crash as a mast and sail go overboard, a rumour flying that the ship is going down, people scared a disease like cholera will break out or fire will start from a candle, a cabin passenger behaving badly by talking to steerage people, a fight among steerage passengers. All this before they have their last looks at England. When things quieten, cabin passengers can hold debates. A hot topic is, Is colonisation good for England?

A few ships are chased and nearly caught by pirates. A crew mutinies. A captain calls in to Cape Town to let four fight duels although the duellists decide not to fight. Passengers are excited when a sailor shoots a porpoise and the cook serves it like beef.

The first sight of New Zealand shocks some. Deserted land, hills, scrub, bush instead of gentle English meadows with stone walls. Even the more open South Island poses problems. Bracken fern and tutu, flax, toetoe, matagouri that needs burning off. Two men go in a whaleboat up Lake Wakatipu to scout land for a sheep-run. Two weeks later they stagger back. Rats ate their food, scrub ripped their clothes, they are both sick with dysentery and do not want to be sheep-farmers any more.

Not everyone stays. Those who do may have to depend on Māori food. Females do it hard — helping to build houses and gardens and fences, chop down trees, cook on open fires, have children, act as medics.

Yet ships keep coming from Britain. A reason settlers uproot themselves is the promise of owning their own land. It is why settlers are described as land-hungry and land-grabbing. The recruitment agents have told them New Zealand has a lot of spare land. Land-buyers give blankets, muskets, tobacco, iron pots, soap, hunting rifles, gunpowder, fish-hooks, tomahawks, spades, steel axes, mirrors, clothing for land. They think they now own it. They do not expect that some Māori might think they are just letting British people settle on land or use it but it is still Māori land. They do not know that land is Papatūānuku, an ancestor, that some iwi and hapū hold that their ancestors did not come from over the sea but sprang from Aotearoa, that no individual owns land. The musket wars and resulting movement that confuse many land rights, now get mixed up with settlers negotiating with Māori for land.

After 1840, Government, which is Governor plus a few officials, makes laws about land. It sets up a special department to stop settlers taking land illegally, appoints a special Protector to Māori, sets up a special Commission to check out land-buying before the Treaty such as crazy claims like an Australian who has never been to New Zealand claiming he owns millions of acres in the South Island.

## Mahi Skills

1. **Local history:** Each iwi and hapū has its own pre-European history with land and most settlers have a different cultural attitude to land. This is not to say settlers never develop a spiritual relationship with it. See if you can find out any early relationships with land in your local area.

2. **Whakataukī:** Whatungarongaro te tangata toitū te whenua translates as As man disappears from sight, the land remains. Explain what it means.

3. **Graph analysis:** Make your own copy of this graph and give it a title and a key. Under it write notes about what it shows.

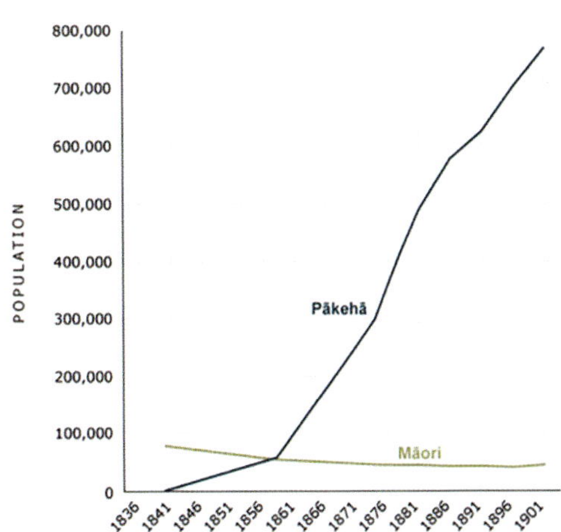


4. **Weighing pros and cons:** You live in England in 1840 and your family is thinking of immigrating to New Zealand. Make a list of pros and cons.

5. **Creating notes:** A chief who sells land to the New Zealand Company for the Wellington settlement says he thought there would be only a few Pākehā who would be traders under his protection. Now he wonders if the whole white tribe is coming. Prepare notes on different attitudes to land of Māori and Pākehā at this time.

ISBN: 9780170462419 PHOTOCOPYING OF THIS PAGE IS RESTRICTED UNDER LAW. 

# 14 Preparing for Power Struggle

**Historians outline some basics of topics to try to make it easier to understand complicated events such as the coming power struggle of the New Zealand Wars.**

Historians do not always agree on a start date and finish date for the wars. A general timeframe can be the early 1840s to the late 1870s. The wars do not go on all the time. There may be a battle, such as a pā assault, and then a longer spell of uneasy peace. Skirmishes are short bursts of fighting when enemy groups come across each other or carry out a fast action such as a raid on a building or an ambush of carts carrying supplies. Campaigns are a series of organised actions such as chasing enemy groups and destroying their shelters and food supplies.

Most fighting is in the North Island — Bay of Islands, Wellington, Whanganui, Taranaki, Waikato, Tauranga, Ōpōtiki, Poverty Bay, Hawke's Bay, Taupō, Te Urewera, Whakatāne. The Wairau Affray is the only South Island conflict.

*Storming Ruapekapeka, 1846.*

Soldiers attack a pā.

During the wars, Nelson, Canterbury and Otago settlements provide food for the north. Nelson gives safety for some refugees. Government sends some Māori prisoners to the South Island. Settlers worry that Māori might take utu for what is happening to relatives in the North. Some Māori at Kaiapoi write letters to newspapers to show they are not going to start attacking Pākehā. South Islanders depend on mail so war news is days old before it gets to Nelson and weeks old before it gets to Dunedin. Many South Island Pākehā begin to say, Where is the money coming from to fight these wars that are stopping development in the colony because immigrants are too scared to come? It is not right we have to pay for things that will help only the North. Perhaps, they say, now is a good time to separate the two islands.

Local iwi and hapū have their own names for events and places in the wars. Early historians looking for one name to cover all the events use Land Wars, Māori Wars, Te Riri Pākehā. The New Zealand Wars are seen by many to show wars are fought in Aotearoa and does not try to pin down just one cause or blame just one group. For some Māori in north Taranaki, Ngā Pakanga Whenua o Mua means conflicts on land in years gone by. Some people now call the wars Ngā Pakanga o Aotearoa. For some Māori, the wars always mean land wars because land is everything and fighting for the right to rule themselves always comes back to the land.

Māori and British culture are used to warfare. Gifts exchanged by rangatira and British sovereigns are often weapons. Ngāpuhi leader Tītore Tākiri, who signs the letter to King William in 1831, sends gifts to the King including pounamu mere and the King sends him suits of armour.

Iwi and hapū keep their own histories of this time and pass them down the generations. Some eyewitness accounts are given such as the description of the Ōrākau battle presented by Hitiri Te Paerata at Parliament on 4 August 1888. British Parliamentary Papers and Journals of the New Zealand Parliament have official government reports. Pamphlets detail meetings such as one between a Pākehā official and some Māori leaders where Rewi Maniapoto declares he will stop fighting. The Army has lists of forces and officers. Military leaders make official reports. The Navy keeps records and accounts such as those of the commander of HMS *Eclipse* which transports troops, dispatches and the Governor during the wars.

ISBN: 9780170462419 PHOTOCOPYING OF THIS PAGE IS RESTRICTED UNDER LAW. 

*Auckland from Britomart army barracks, 1852.*

British and New Zealand newspapers publish stories in English although some are wildly inaccurate. Māori language newspapers are published by Government, missionaries, Pākehā sponsors and Māori groups. Historians write accounts such as James Cowan's book about Kimble Kent who deserts his British Regiment, lives with Taranaki Māori and gets caught up in their war. Government pays James Cowan to write a history of the wars. A Pākehā who speaks te reo Māori, he interviews Māori and Pākehā to get their stories. His father fights in the Waikato War and the family farm is on land taken from Māori. Later James is adviser for the silent film *Rewi's Last Stand*. The producer remakes it with sound and casts descendants of Māori and Pākehā who fought in the wars.

Many soldiers are illiterate, but some who can read and write keep diaries, write letters or books, leave private papers behind. Soldier artists paint or sketch events and people. Some settlers write books. British leaders, impressed by pā designs, sketch them. Some private letters survive, such as those of Maria Nicholson who is a nanny in Taranaki. Māori write letters to Māori and Pākehā.

There are no neutral people checking facts to make sure stories are accurate. Official Crown records have gaps. Some people do not want to officially record their decisions or events. Some records are lost or destroyed by disasters such as fires. Many events are controversial when they happen and remain so today. This is why it is sometimes safest to say, This is said to have happened.



PHOTOCOPYING OF THIS PAGE IS RESTRICTED UNDER LAW. ISBN: 9780170462419

Another big question is, What does New Zealand look like at this time? Very different to today, is the short answer. Fighters have to be fit, strong and brave to cope with the terrain – dense bush, swamps, creeks and hills; few roads or tracks. No hotels to supply meals and beds. When war breaks out in the 1840s it is up to the Governor to deal with it. Letters to and from London can take months by ship. New Zealand Company settlements will grow into towns – Wellington, Whanganui, New Plymouth, Nelson, Dunedin, Christchurch. In the 1840s they are isolated from each other and surrounded by Māori pā and kāinga, bush and forest. Some later towns including Hamilton and Tauranga begin as military posts. New Zealand's population is strung out and small. It will not get to even one million until 1908.

## Mahi Skills

1 **Local history:** a) People have argued over Wanganui versus Whanganui for years. Find out which spelling has no meaning in te reo Māori and which spelling has traditions in oral history. b) Wellington gets its name from the Duke of Wellington. Find out Māori names for the area.

2 **Map-reading:** Explain what the map suggests about New Zealand's natural features at that time.

3 **Being unbiased:** Choose the name for the wars that you see as unbiased – being neutral, and not taking sides or passing judgement. Be prepared to justify your choice.

4 **Indicating:** Print or sketch an outline map of New Zealand. Indicate generally the areas of conflict during the wars.

5 **Linking movies:** Movies to do with the wars include *River Queen*, *Utu*, *The Te Kooti Trail*. Choose one, or another, to research and decide why historians would regard it as a secondary rather than primary source.

# 15 Fighters in the New Zealand Wars

**Historians know that being a fighter for rangatiratanga and a fighter for sovereignty means different military approaches and organisations. Also belonging to differently-sized military outfits. Some experts say Lieutenant-General Duncan Cameron's force for the Waikato equals an army of one million invading New Zealand today.**

After the Treaty, Britain stations troops in New Zealand. They are paid professionals that Britain can send to any colonies. When war breaks out, the Governor pens letters to the Colonial Office asking for more soldiers, and each Governor keeps asking for more soldiers. British soldiers do most of the fighting against Māori. They are called British forces or imperial forces or Crown forces. In the 1860s Britain starts withdrawing troops. It is up to you to provide your own troops, it tells the New Zealand Government. The forces that the New Zealand Government provides are called colonial forces or government forces or Crown forces. Their armed constables of the Armed Constabulary act as both soldiers and police. Militia are settlers whose names are on a list so if they are needed to fight they can be called up. Volunteers are members of the public who offer to fight.

Forest Rangers are specialists whose weapons include knives, pistols and sabres. They travel light to ambush Māori war parties in the forest, especially at night. A famous member is Gustavus Ferdinand von Tempsky whose death is pictured on the cover of this book. He has a pointed beard and long hair in ringlets, and gets a reputation for being a brave and popular leader. Māori call him Manurau, bird that flits everywhere. The Flying Arawa Column are young Te Arawa specialists who fight Māori guerrillas. Gilbert Mair, who learns te reo Māori at his father's kauri gum business, is a commander. He is in Rotorua when a force of 600 Waikato Māori march to help Tauranga Māori. He begins recruiting for the Flying Arawa Column. The first man wanting to join is a grey-haired active and brave tattooed warrior of about seventy. When Mair tells him he is too old, the warrior does war dances, insists he can run through forest without shaking dewdrops from leaves, and demands a gun. Mair is impressed but does not hire him.

Some Māori groups fight alongside Crown forces; some fight without Crown forces against Māori fighting the Crown forces. These Māori are called kūpapa, Queenites, friendlies or the Native Contingent. Native at this time is the official word for Māori. Te Rangihiwinui Keepa, later known as Te Keepa or Major Kemp, is a Pūtiki rangatira and leader of the Whanganui Native Contingent. He is said to be a great sight on an unsaddled horse in his cloak and kilt with cartridge belts, revolvers, sword, tomahawk and rifle. One man who often serves with Te Keepa's warriors, barefoot like them, is Pākehā-Māori Thomas Adamson. He is a scout with stamina, strength and bushcraft.


PHOTOCOPYING OF THIS PAGE IS RESTRICTED UNDER LAW.
ISBN: 9780170462419

*HMS* North Star *firing at Ōtuihu pā.*

However, different hapū and iwi will have different terms. For example, kūpapa starts off as those Māori who are not involved and morphs into Māori who are friendly to the Crown. Some kūpapa fight because they are traditional rivals of other iwi and hapū fighting the Crown. Some fight because they think it is the best way to hold on to their land. Some historians suggest Christian Māori may feel religion makes a bond between them and settlers. There are some rewards for kūpapa. The Governor can give annuities (yearly fixed sums of money) or gifts to chiefs. For example, when Tāmati Wāka Nene writes to the Governor in June 1846 and asks for money to buy a cart, the Governor orders the money be sent to Nene.

Historians estimate that in total about 4000 warriors, a third of those available, fight Crown forces. Not as a professional united army with ranks and specialist groups but as iwi and hapū groups under their own rangatira with maybe rūnanga in the middle of a battle to talk about tactics and warriors going home to manage food production for iwi and hapū. They might help other iwi or hapū, but even when Māori elect a Māori King in the late 1850s, warriors do not join together in a united army. When Rewi Maniapoto supports the Māori King and is part of a Kīngitanga fighting force, he is always a member of Ngāti Maniapoto. Some Māori wear a flax maro apron or piupiu kilt and cloak; some wear Pākehā dress or a mix-and-match.

Outnumbered and without heavy fire-power, warriors have a big weapon — local knowledge. They know everything about the terrain down to how to treat wounds with boiled flax root juice and dock-root, how to smear red ochre to keep insects away. Compare that to a soldier who has just arrived in the country, has never met a Māori, has no map, who keeps losing his cap and ripping his uniform and getting tripped up as he struggles through bush with weapon, rations, blanket, coat, cooking gear and maybe a cannon or mortar shell. How silently and swiftly Māori glide through the same bush and just melt away, he will think. A few Crown soldiers desert and fight for Māori. One is an Irishman called Charles Kane. Māori later kill him as a suspected traitor.

Children help build pā and do jobs such as carrying water and ammunition to warriors. Artists and writers tend to concentrate on male fighters. Yet some Māori females fight and accounts reveal some fight for the Crown. One known as Queen Victoria fights in the Whanganui district and is first to enter Wereroa pā when Crown troops storm it. Te Arawa woman Hēni Te Kiri Karamū fights on the Crown side with her uncle. One day she nails a long-range shot that kills a warrior in a waka. Tuta Nihoniho, Ngāti Porou rangatira, says of his mother Heeni Nohowaka, When going into action she wore two cartridge-belts and carried a single-barrel percussion-lock gun. Major von Tempsky says the Native Contingent includes women who carry heavy loads, act as hewers of wood and drawers of water, cook, and frequently fight with the most determined bravery ... Upon the field of battle these ladies are perfect amazons and thoroughly despise the man who in the hour of danger would exhibit either fear or cowardice.

Māori build many new pā to encourage soldiers to attack and so some are never used. Gunfighter pā features include trenches, earth walls, wooden palisades, fighting stages, tunnels, anti-artillery bunkers, hidden rifle pits, escape routes, space for supplies and natural defences such as cliffs. They are usually on sites that are almost impossible to surround but have an exposed front to tempt the enemy to attack there. Some pā are built quickly. It takes 80 men only one night to build the pā at Waitara. This makes it easy to abandon pā; another reason is pā where blood has been spilled are tapu. If supplies run out, people might leave during battles, often at night. Soldiers may spend days bombarding and attacking a pā only to find it empty, and soon Māori put up another hard-to-get-at pā at another location. Māori call muskets ngutu pārera. They like two-barrel shotguns loaded with musket balls that can fire twice before reloading. They call them tūpara, two barrels. Females may go with the men to reload. Guns have mana and warriors often carve the wooden butts.

*War council.*

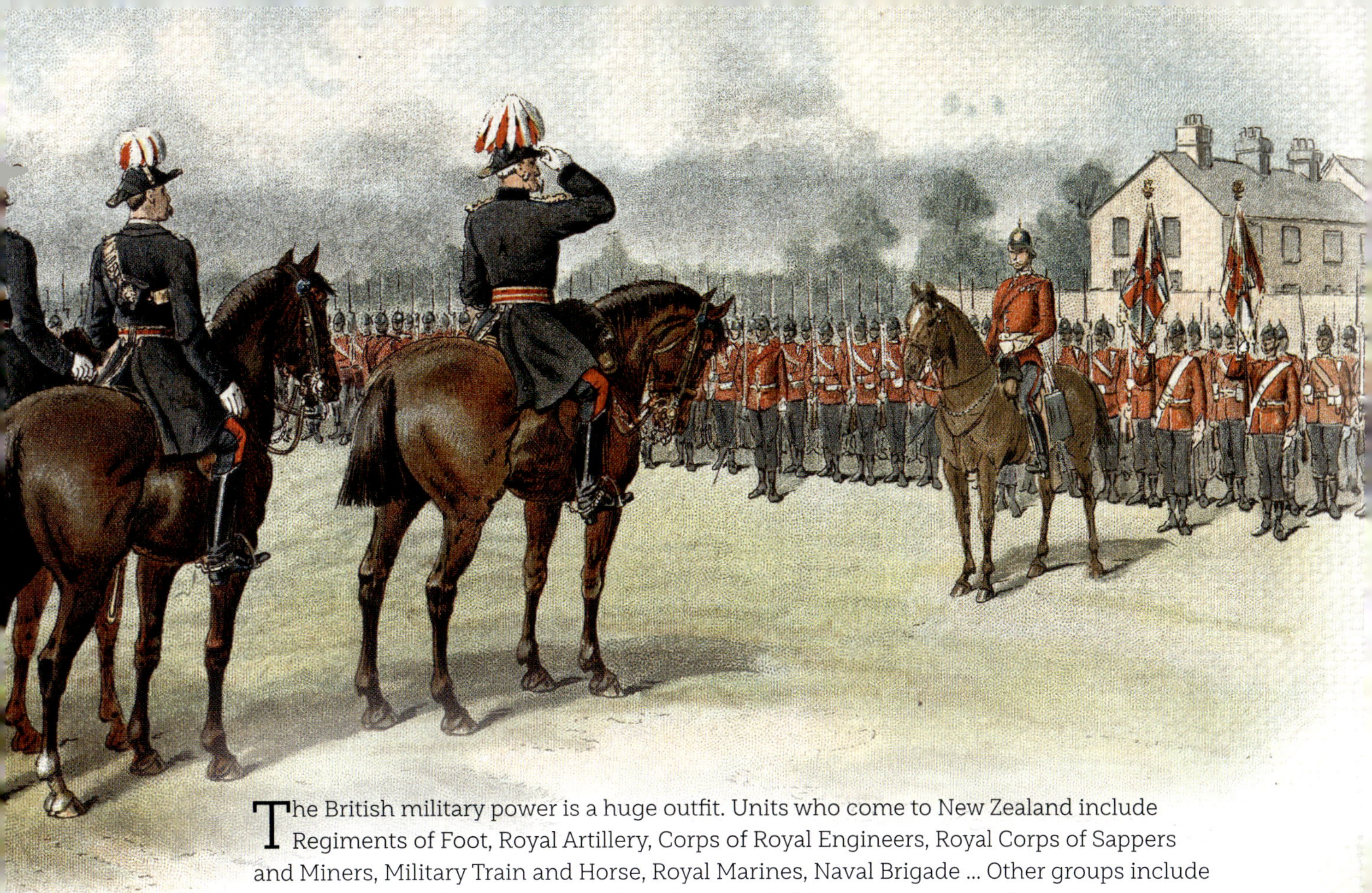

The British military power is a huge outfit. Units who come to New Zealand include Regiments of Foot, Royal Artillery, Corps of Royal Engineers, Royal Corps of Sappers and Miners, Military Train and Horse, Royal Marines, Naval Brigade ... Other groups include spies, scouts, guides, advisers, cooks, labourers. Soldiers wear caps, tunics and trousers although some ditch them for cloaks and kilts. In their red jackets, and even their blue jackets, with white bandoliers making a cross formation on the soldier's back and front, they look as if they are showing enemies where to shoot. Many soldiers have heavy beards.

Artillery are their big guns. Cannon, usually mounted on wheels, fire different-size balls. The newly-invented Armstrong gun arrives in New Zealand. Howitzers and mortars fire shells. The Congreve rocket tube is filled with gunpowder which burns to make the rocket fly. Soldiers have high-quality muskets. The Crown has a fleet of armed and armoured steam ships to move troops, weapons and supplies. Imagine waka going up against a steamer on the Waikato River. Crown ships bombard pā, carry troops and equipment, evacuate settlers and serve as hospitals. Marines and sailors may go ashore to fight.

*British Army camp, New Zealand, 1860s.*

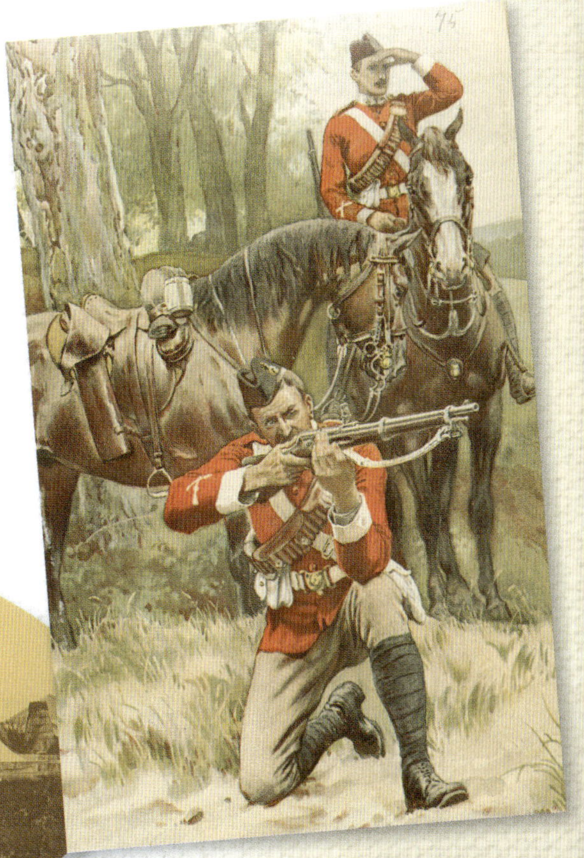

*The British Government is used to sending its army and navy to squash unrest in its Empire.*

Troops get rations – usually bread, meat fresh or salted, rum, tea, coffee, sugar, pepper and salt. In camp, cooks make meals; in bush, soldiers get their own. Ramrods are good for roasting birds over a fire. Crown forces supply Māori allies and Māori supply Crown forces, such as women carrying kits of cooked potatoes to sentries on camp duty. Even in the bush, soldiers keep up traditions such as saluting, hoisting the Union Jack, marching to flute, fife (small, shrill flute) and drum. Away from camps, they sleep in churches and churchyards, tents, ti-tree and raupō and flax shelters. Settlers know that once soldiers turn up, everything edible or usable disappears. At Waimate Mission Station soldiers come to camp; they kill missionary livestock and poultry, and use fences and roof shingles for firewood. On land, soldiers carry heavy gear such as tents and artillery on packhorses or bullock-drawn drays hired from settlers. In the bush there is smoke from tobacco and cooking fires, and the smell of cordite (powder used in guns). Soldiers wade or swim across rivers holding weapons high. If he is lucky, a wounded soldier might have a horse-drawn ambulance wagon take him to a surgeon in a military hospital in a settlement, or a mobile hospital behind the fighting area. Redoubts have earthworks and ditches like pā and can be put up quickly and even under enemy fire. There is space for many men, tents, magazines to store ammunition, a hospital, guards. Stockades are usually of thick wood with loopholes to shoot through. Troops can live in them, store weapons and ammunition, and settlers can shelter in them. Blockhouses have one or two storeys with loopholes and stand alone, or are part of stockades. Saps are trenches so soldiers can get to pā.

Army life can be tough. Bad pay, bad drinking habits, bad punishments, public floggings, bad officers who buy their titles. Soldiers are taught to obey without argument but records show some begin to question the rightness of the wars they are asked to fight in New Zealand.

## Mahi Skills

1 **Local history:** Māori return von Tempsky's sword to his wife after his death. Some British soldiers stay after their term of service is finished and marry Māori females. Describe how relationships between locals and outsiders can be made in war.

2 **Presentation:** British Governors involved in the New Zealand Wars are William Hobson, Robert FitzRoy, George Grey, Thomas Gore Browne, George Bowen. Choose one and prepare a short presentation in any form about him. Or instead prepare a short presentation about Hūria Mātenga who is an example of how life goes on as usual in some areas while another area is involved in a battle. She is one of local Māori who dive time and time again into wild seas to rescue crew and passengers when the *Delaware* is wrecked in 1863 on rocks near Nelson.

3 **Thinking about terms:** In 1947 Government changes the official term Native to Māori. Suggest reasons and check how accurate you are.

4 **Impact on animals:** Most soldiers are infantry foot-soldiers, but there is also cavalry – men on horses. In just the first four months of 1864, 1000 horses are shipped in. Māori also use horses. Te Kooti and his men ride, and capture many more from the enemy. Abandoned or runaway horses may have begun the wild horses in the Kaimanawa Mountains. Explain how animals get caught up in human wars.

5 **Crucial features:** Crucial means so important it can decide success or failure. Māori have a long history with the land of New Zealand and British with the land of Britain. Explain how that is a crucial feature.


PHOTOCOPYING OF THIS PAGE IS RESTRICTED UNDER LAW.
ISBN: 9780170462419

# Wairau Affray 16

**Some historians see the Wairau Affray as the first serious conflict between Māori and British after the Treaty. At the time settlers call it a brutal slaughter, and blame Māori for being lawless. Today, historians call it an affray, a group or groups fighting in public and disturbing the peace. It is seen as a power struggle over a specific block of land and over government and organisation.**

The New Zealand Company settlement of Nelson has over 500 British settlers. Many want land. Wairau Valley has fertile plains. The Company claims it has bought it. Te Rauparaha and his Ngāti Toa followers, who got control of it from Rangitāne iwi, say the Company has not bought it. One story has a Sydney mariner persuading Te Rauparaha to sign an agreement for what Te Rauparaha thinks are rights to timber and water, but are actually rights to Wairau Plains land, in exchange for a cannon. The agreement is sold to Colonel William Wakefield. Te Rauparaha is said to be furious when he discovers the cheat. He rips the agreement up, says he has not sold the land although he lets people cross it, camp on it and take wood from it. No surveyors though. Another story has local whaler Jacky Guard giving the cannon to Te Rauparaha's brother Nohorua for the right to set up a whaling station at Kākāpō Bay. The mariner is said to have taken the cannon and used it to pay for the Wairau deal.

*Te Rangihaeata.*

The New Zealand Company sends in surveyors early in 1843. Te Rauparaha and Te Rangihaeata go to Nelson to talk to Company man Arthur Wakefield. They want the official in charge of investigating land-buying to look into the issue. I will when I've finished the job I'm on, the official says. Rangatira who occupy the land go to Nelson. Te Rauparaha has no right to sell the land, they say. A standoff. Ngāti Toa order the survey to be stopped. William Wakefield tells brother Arthur to continue it. Ngāti Toa evict surveyors, remove pegs, burn huts. The British, despite warnings not to, decide to arrest Te Rauparaha and Te Rangihaeata on arson charges. The Government brings a party of nearly 50 to Cloudy Bay including Arthur Wakefield, and Police Magistrate Henry Thompson who is described as angry and having fits of rage where he tears his beard out and his face turns red. Many men they lead have little or no training in how to act in such a situation or how to handle weapons. On 17 June the party goes up Tuamarina Stream to where Te Rauparaha and Te Rangihaeata with about 90 Māori including women and children are. I am arresting you for burning down huts, says the Police Magistrate. The huts were made from rushes surveyors took off my land so I burned my own property, answers Te Rauparaha. The Police Magistrate

ISBN: 9780170462419 PHOTOCOPYING OF THIS PAGE IS RESTRICTED UNDER LAW.

Wairau Valley.

tries to handcuff Te Rauparaha. An insult to mana. I am on my own land and Māori don't go to England to take British land, shouts Te Rangihaeata. A musket shot, confused fighting, some British dead and some fatally wounded, two Māori dead. One is Te Rongo, a wife of Rangihaeata and said to be a daughter of Te Rauparaha. The British retreat; four more are killed. Those who have not escaped are surrounded and forced to surrender. Te Rangihaeata claims utu for his wife. With his mere he, and others, kill nine British including Wakefield and the Police Magistrate. Four Māori dead and three wounded. Twenty-two British dead and five wounded.

Governor Robert FitzRoy arrives in December. The official view is Ngāti Toa were provoked by reckless actions of the New Zealand Company. I will make sure, he says, that not an acre, not an inch of land belonging to the natives shall be touched without their consent. He conducts a one-man inquiry into the event. The white men were in the wrong and had no right to survey land and build houses, he says. The chiefs committed a horrible crime in murdering men who had surrendered. British and Māori must live peaceably with no more bloodshed. The Colonial Office approves. It does not want expensive military action against Ngāti Toa. Settlers are furious. They say, Government is favouring Māori over us. When they hear FitzRoy has been recalled to Britain, they burn an effigy (rough model) of him. An 1844 investigation says Wairau Valley has not been legally sold. Government is to pay compensation to Rangitāne iwi who are considered original owners. In 1847 Governor Grey demands Wairau be sold to the Crown.

## Mahi Skills

1. **Local history:** When the cannon involved fired, it shook the ground so got called Puhuriwhenua. It still exists. Find out where and what it is like.
2. **Toning it down:** This event used to be known as Wairau Massacre, and the site as Massacre Hill. Suggest reasons for the change of name.
3. **Missing info:** State what additional material you would include and why if you had a lot more space. Cultural clash? Maps? Illustrations?
4. **Resource analysis:** Explain the attraction of Wairau to settlers.
5. **Local knowledge:** When the Government ship arrives at Cloudy Bay people assume it has brought the land investigator. The local missionary hears who it has brought instead, and writes in his journal, *Surely not, this will be the height of madness, but I cannot believe it. They will never suffer themselves to be made prisoners.* Explain what he means and what it suggests of the importance of local knowledge and tikanga.

# Northern War Erupts

17

**Historians look at pivotal characters whose actions spark off effects and other people seem to wheel around them. Hōne Heke signing the Treaty maybe stirs things up because some rangatira may not want to sign below him. Now he chops down a flagpole and helps cause a split and a continuing sensitive issue among Ngāpuhi through his and rangatira Wāka Nene's involvement in war.**

Governor Hobson looks for a place to set up a government. Okiato will be a good capital, he thinks. Close to Kororāreka, and a rangatira has sold land to a British merchant for a trading station there. He shifts his family there. Officials, troops, settlers come to live in buildings and tents. Then Ngāti Whatua chiefs offer Hobson land for a capital on the shores of Waitematā Harbour. Auckland is tiny but growing, is more central, with harbours, rivers, fertile land, water supplies, good climate, space. Hobson shifts down and Auckland becomes the new capital in March 1841. Up north, Ngāpuhi have questions. Why does the Governor insult Ngāpuhi like this after we set up a relationship with the British? Why do our traditional enemies have the Governor at their place? Why is the Governor closer to the waka middle when a rangatira sits at the back? Why are so few ships coming to the Bay? Why has demand for our timber and produce dried up? Why is it harder to get Pākehā goods? Why are our settlers and traders going to live in Auckland? Why are the British forcing people to pay customs duties which make things like tobacco expensive? Why does money paid by ships to visit a port now go to the British? Why doesn't the Governor come back when we ask?

ISBN: 9780170462419
PHOTOCOPYING OF THIS PAGE IS RESTRICTED UNDER LAW.

Hōne Heke becomes spokesman for this unrest. He writes letters to the Governor. He hoped the Treaty would help his people but now times are hard. His mana is threatened by rules which stop him charging fees on ships entering the Bay and tolls for crossing his land. Māori are losing land to the Crown and becoming slaves. The British flag is a symbol of this. The Governor should come and see him so they can meet face to face and decide what is best to be done. No need for soldiers. The Governor can take down the flagpole and put up two side by side for the British flag and the Māori flag.

*Hone Heke (centre), wife Hariata Rongo (daughter of Hongi Hika and Turikatuku), Te Ruki Kawiti.*

At daybreak on 8 July 1844 Heke's men cut down the flagpole. Heke writes to the Governor again. The flagpole belonged to me. I made it for the Māori flag and it was never paid for. In late August the Governor travels to the Bay and goes to a missionary-organised hui at Waimate. Hōne Heke does not go. Some Ngāpuhi rangatira, including Tāmati Wāka Nene, go. Even though they are upset at British actions they want peace, want the Governor to send soldiers away, think chopping down the flagpole was a bad idea, and they will keep Heke in order. Nene will say of Heke, This man laughed at all our persuasions and threats and we are older than him. The British replace the flagpole. On 9–10 January 1845 Heke's men chop it down.

The Governor issues a bounty of 100 pounds for Heke's capture. He has the flagpole replaced. On 19 January Heke's men chop it down. The British replace it. They put iron around it, build a blockhouse beside it and put guards in it. They put wooden palisades around it all. They put Kororāreka on alert. They put a warship in the bay. Its armed marines and sailors are ready to fight.

Heke has been looking around Northland for support. Kawiti is a warrior chief of Ngāti Hine hapū. Trained in warfare and leadership, he fights in the musket wars but develops a reputation as peace-maker. At Waitangi he argues against a treaty but signs later. Pākehā call him The Duke – Te Ruki. (The Duke of Wellington is one of the most famous British military leaders of all time.) He has fighting pā but likes to chase enemies and fight hand-to-hand. Heke sends Kawiti a greenstone mere, said to have human waste on it. The message is, British are disrespecting Ngāpuhi mana. Kawiti agrees to join him. Before dawn on 11 March 1845 Kawiti and his men attack the armed marines and sailors stationed ashore at Kororāreka. Heke and his men kill the soldiers in the blockhouse and attack the flagpole, getting it down at about 10 am. Skirmishing follows.


PHOTOCOPYING OF THIS PAGE IS RESTRICTED UNDER LAW.
ISBN: 9780170462419

The British order the settlers to evacuate to ships which head to Auckland. Suddenly the town's magazine, housing gunpowder in barrels, explodes. An accident or a move to stop Māori getting gunpowder? Buildings catch fire. Soldiers evacuate to ships. The warship fires shots into town. There is looting and destruction of the town although Heke is said to draw an imaginary line and order nothing be destroyed beyond it. The churches are saved. The British are said to have had about 20 killed and 23 wounded, and Māori about 13 dead and 28 wounded. The British are shocked. Will Heke and Kawiti attack Auckland next? Governor FitzRoy asks for more soldiers to be sent.

## Mahi Skills

1 **Local history:** Hobson changes the name Okiato to Russell after Lord Russell who is British Secretary of State for the Colonies. Kororāreka is part of the port of Russell and British call it Russell also. Today, Kororāreka is also known as Russell while Okiato has its Māori name although sometimes people call it Old Russell. See if making a diagram of this lessens the confusion of trying to understand it.

2 **Letters as primary sources:** Hōne Heke says in a letter to the Governor: ... *do you return to your own country, to England which was made by God for you. God made this land for us and not for any stranger or foreign Nation to touch.* Explain why it is a primary source and then put his message into your own words.

3 **Using a timeline:** A timeline is a way of showing important events in the order they happen. Kawiti is said to have been born only five years after Captain Cook circumnavigated New Zealand. Make a timeline of those two events and the Wairau Affray and the beginning of the Northern War. Then make a second timeline to show the chopping down of the flagpole.

4 **Thinking of economic matters:** One of the matters contributing to conflict in the northern region is how its economy is declining for Māori. Give some examples and suggest reasons for this.

5 **Pivotal characters:** Read the following about how pivotal characters interact and choose one to find out more about.

*Hōne Heke fights on the beach at Kororāreka in 1830 at the start of The Girls' War between northern and southern Ngāpuhi. Young Māori girls insulting each other blows up into battles when hundreds of warriors get involved and it takes several years for muru to be sorted out. The girls include past and present girlfriends of Pākehā whaler Brind, who will later father Isabella who is murdered at Motuarohia Island. A reason rangatira pass Maketū over to British justice is said to be to prevent iwi warfare erupting over Isabella's death. The grandfather of Isabella is Rewa, one of the chiefs who write to King William IV in 1831. Rewa signs the Treaty but then tries to stop others signing. In a letter to a British trader, Rewa says, We are not like the King of England; we are all chiefs here. He becomes a protector of the Catholic mission and during the Northern War offers to help defend 'his whites'.*

 PHOTOCOPYING OF THIS PAGE IS RESTRICTED UNDER LAW. 

# 18 Northern War

**Historians look at how people stick up for what they think are their rights and how governments react. Government and Pākehā generally at this time call Heke and Kawiti rebels because the chiefs do not agree with how Government thinks things should be. Today many say the Northern War is not a rebellion as much as a protest. Heke wants the British to listen to Ngāpuhi grievances. He is not insisting settlers and Government leave. He wants them to honour the Treaty. He says it is not his chopping down the flagpole that causes war but Government's putting it up again. His quarrel is with the Governor and not settlers. But now there is war, not the partnership Ngāpuhi wanted when they signed the Treaty.**

*Battle at Puketutu pā, near Ōkaihau.*

Hōne Heke and Kawiti versus British soldiers. But Heke has also got offside with Tāmati Wāka Nene who will give support and advice to the British. Skirmishing between the two Ngāpuhi groups continues on and off until peace. They are said have some understandings – no ambushes, no fighting at night.

At the end of April, a ship brings 470 British soldiers and 50 volunteers to the Bay of Islands. They decide to attack Pōmare II's Ōtuihu pā. Pōmare has much mana and did not help in the attack on Kororāreka. But someone tells the Governor that Pōmare is stockpiling gunpowder and ammunition for Hōne Heke. Several troop ships and a ship with cannon sail up Kawakawa River and anchor off Ōtuihu. The British persuade Pōmare to come aboard and take him prisoner. Soldiers go into Ōtuihu. They find a lot of ducks, turkeys and pigs but no gunpowder or ammunition. The soldiers loot stores and set the pā on fire.

Heke begins building Puketutu pā on the shores of Lake Ōmāpere.

Over 200 British soldiers do a four-day march to it. Rough going with no tents and rain wrecking their supplies. When they get to the pā on 8 May they see they should have dragged big guns in. They try Congreve rockets. Only one hits the pā and it does little damage. Soldiers advance. Kawiti and his men come out of the bush to fight hand-to-hand. Heke's men join in. After hours of skirmishing, Māori abandon the pā. The British occupy it. Reports say there are 15–28 British dead and 40 wounded. Māori deaths are higher. Kawiti loses a son. Next day the British march off.


PHOTOCOPYING OF THIS PAGE IS RESTRICTED UNDER LAW.
ISBN: 9780170462419

*Ruapekapeka pā, British soldiers, raupō tents.*

On 15 May in the dark, soldiers go up Waikare Inlet in boats to attack Te Kapotai pā. They believe they will find loot from Kororāreka. Te Kapotai withdraw. There is fighting in the bush, mostly between Te Kapotai and Ngāpuhi, who are after utu for defeat by Te Kapotai about 30 years ago. Soldiers loot and burn the pā. They do not find items from Kororāreka.

Heke's home pā of Te Ahuahu (Pukenui) is inland. Nene and his men move inland to a pā at Ōkaihau. Nene is unhappy that Heke accuses him of fighting for blankets. On 12 June 1845 Heke and most of his men are away gathering food. His enemy, Hokianga chief Te Taonui, backed up by Nene, seizes the pā. Heke gathers about 500 fighters. The two forces battle it out on the lower slopes. Te Taonui and Nene are outnumbered but stop Heke's forces. Heke has a thigh wound and his men carry him away.

Kawiti and Pene Taui turn Ōhaeawai pā into a gunfighter pā. Six hundred and fifteen soldiers with several cannon set out from Waimate Mission Station. Ōhaeawai is only six miles away but it takes a long time to carry artillery, ammunition and supplies. When food runs short, Nene gives them beef, potatoes and flour. They arrive at Ōhaeawai on 24 June. Their leader, Colonel Despard, has not seen active combat for about 30 years and has gout. When Nene earlier visits him with an offer to help, the reply is, When I want the help of savages, I will ask for it. It is said the interpreter does not translate that for Nene.

Soldiers set up gun batteries. They open fire. The guns are too small to destroy the pā. On 30 June a 32-pounder cannon arrives. Soldiers put it in the hilltop gun battery and begin firing. Māori from the pā attack the battery, kill the sentry, take down the Union Jack. Soldiers recapture the position. Back in the pā, Māori put the Union Jack on a flagpole under their own flag. Soldiers attack. Māori wait to the last minute and open fire through holes in the trench roof. Soldiers bombard until 9 July when the defenders leave in the night. British records show Māori leave all arms taken from soldiers and some of their own guns, ammunition and tomahawks, pototoes and Indian corn. Soldiers remove it all and burn the pā. But it is a defeat for the British with 41 dead and 73 wounded. Some people say Māori invent trench warfare there.

Kawiti spends several months building the strongest pā yet in the north. It is called Ruapekapeka because its trenches, underground tunnels and bombproof shelters make it look like a bats' nest. A British force of about 1300, and a Māori force of about 400 under Nene, set off to attack. It takes them several weeks to drag heavy artillery about 12 miles. They camp and set up firing positions. Heke arrives with men but Māori are still outnumbered. On 10 January 1846 the British start bombarding. It creates legends such as children defusing shells. Next day scouts report that only Kawiti and some warriors are inside the pā. Where are the others? Church service? Sheltering from the bombardment? Hoping to ambush soldiers in bush outside? Has the pā done its job by making soldiers waste time and energy to get to it and attack it for nothing? The British launch an assault. Pā inhabitants go into the bush. After heavy fighting, Māori take Kawiti away. More heavy shooting among trees although soldiers will not be lured into bush. Twelve British soldiers and an unknown number of Māori are killed. Māori slip away into bush. Firing eventually fizzles out. The Governor claims a victory.

About a week later, Heke, Kawiti and Nene meet at a pā of a neutral chief and agree to seek peace. Two years later Heke meets the Governor at Waimate North mission house. He gives him a greenstone mere. It speaks as a symbol – Heke accepts the Governor's right to be in New Zealand but he expects him to honour the Treaty.

*Soldiers camp in front of Ōhaeawai pā.*

## Mahi Skills

1 **Local history:** Show how, in text or diagram or map, this has been for Māori a Ngāpuhi affair and why Ngāpuhi are the holders of its history.

2 **Looking at responses:** Comment on how Hōne Heke and Government respond to the Treaty of Waitangi in different ways.

3 **Facts and opinions:** Make a list of facts and a list of opinions from the following: Some people think Tāmati Wāka Nene wants the Governor to confiscate the lands of Heke and Kawiti and give them to him but no lands are confiscated. The British build Tāmati Wāka Nene a cottage at Kororāreka and give him an annuity. The Governor asks him for advice. When Nene dies, Governor Grey writes in a dispatch to London that Nene did more than any other Māori leader to get the Queen's authority and promote colonisation.

4 **Identifying times:** Identify a time when the following happen:
- verbal disrespect
- a bat's nest is the focus
- British intelligence gets the wrong idea
- a disease causes bad pain
- an item sends a powerful message
- a flag is captured.

5 **Following up:** What happens later in the flagpole story? Find out why 1858 is another important date at Maiki Hill.


PHOTOCOPYING OF THIS PAGE IS RESTRICTED UNDER LAW.
ISBN: 9780170462419

# Wellington War

19

**Historians look at stakeholders – people with interests or concerns. The Wellington area is an example of where interests and concerns of stakeholders lead to war.**

Te Rauparaha and Te Rangihaeata are living in the Wellington district. So are many settlers; 4000 by 1843. Wanting more land, they look at Heretaunga (Hutt Valley). The Land Claims Commissioner is checking land claims there and the New Zealand Company is told not all their land buys are legitimate. The Governor supports settler land claims, and wants to evict Māori from Hutt Valley. There is tension among locals. Te Rangihaeata is against settlers moving in because he says land has not been paid for, and he does not want to talk to the Governor because he hears rumours the Governor wants to hang him. Te Rauparaha agrees Māori should leave Hutt Valley. Local Māori go against both Governor and Te Rauparaha by clearing bush, extending gardens and protesting they have not been compensated for loss of land. The Governor builds redoubts, stockades and outposts and puts in militia until British troops arrive. In February 1846, when settlers begin to move on to land Māori have left and meet resistance from remaining Māori, the Governor sends in a big military force. Ngāti Rangatahi chief Te Kāeaea, of the Hutt River settlement of Maraenuku built in 1842 to show Ngāti Tama claim to the land, gets a threat from the Governor: Leave by noon of the next day or you will be attacked. The chief leaves. Troops march in to Maraenuku, burn houses, wreck the chapel and burial place. Ngāti Rangatahi raid settler farms and wreck furniture, smash windows, kill pigs and threaten to kill settlers if they raise the alarm. The Governor declares martial law – military government. Several hundred settlers take refuge in town. In late March two Māori are put on trial for looting settler homes, and a few days later Māori kill a settler farmer and son working on disputed land.

*Maraenuku pā.*

ISBN: 9780170462419
PHOTOCOPYING OF THIS PAGE IS RESTRICTED UNDER LAW.

Rangatira Tōpine Te Mamaku from Whanganui gets involved. During the musket wars he is sometimes an ally of Te Rauparaha and sometimes an enemy. Now he leads a force of about 200 in a dawn attack on British troops at Boulcott's farm in the Hutt Valley. In the early hours of 16 May the sentry sees Māori crawling through bush and fires at them. Māori kill six soldiers and mortally wound another two. One of the dead is said to be the young bugle boy. Reports, books, poems and newspaper stories will tell of his bravery, how he manages to blow his bugle even though tomahawk blows are hacking him to death, how he holds the bugle between his knees to sound the alarm when his arm is chopped off. Turns out he is a 21-year-old drummer. Newspapers also wrongly say Te Rangihaeata leads the attack. Te Mamaku sends letters to chiefs in Whanganui urging them to come and fight. Some letters are intercepted and forwarded to Government. Rumours fly that the attack on Wellington town will soon start. A month later Māori ambush an armed patrol and mortally wound a soldier.

Although Te Rauparaha encouraged Māori to leave Hutt Valley, Governor Grey does not trust him. In July a naval group goes to his Taupō pā and puts him on their ship. You are under arrest for supplying weapons to Māori who are rebelling against the Crown, they tell him. Te Rangihaeata takes a party to try to get him but is forced to retreat. The British send Te Rauparaha to Auckland and hold him without charge on another naval vessel for ten months. Soldiers go to Te Rangihaeata's pā at Pāuatahanui. He goes into the hills. His new position is now known as Battle Hill. On 6 August 1846 a force of soldiers, militia, armed police, Te Āti Awa and some breakaway Ngāti Toa whom the British do not trust, attack in the cold and rain. The defenders hold firm against thousands of rounds of musket fire. Three soldiers are killed and the attackers pull back. Next day the British drag up two mortars. They fire about 80 shells, then they leave it to Te Āti Awa to launch raids. On 13 August they find the defenders have gone and they chase them into Horowhenua district. On 14 August Te Āti Awa capture a group of Whanganui Māori who have been with Te Rangihaeata. The Governor charges them with rebellion. None speak enough English to defend themselves. They plead guilty and are sentenced to be convicts in Australia. Te Whareaitu is hanged for 'rebellion' at Paremata barracks. He is a Whanganui chief related to Tōpine Te Mamaku and it is thought that even though there is no evidence that Te Whareaitu kills anyone, Governor Grey wants to make an example of him. No soldier is keen to be hangman and the one who does the job is said to drown in shallow water about a year later. While Government in 1847 has Te Rauparaha captured and Te Rangihaeata in exile, it buys Wairau land.

## Mahi Skills

1 **Local history:** List stakeholders in Hutt Valley at this time.

2 **Seeing interconnections:** Show interconnections among stakeholders.

3 **Identifying actions and reasons for them:** Explain who the two groups in the image on page 59 of Maraenuku pā are, what they are doing, and why.

4 **Identifying differences:** Explain the difference between each item in the following pairs: Heretaunga and Maraenuku. Militia and British troops. Raiding and using shells. Battle Hill and Boulcott's farm. Land Claims Commissioner and New Zealand Company.

5 **Giving examples:** Comment on how the bugle-boy incident is an example of misinformation and find an image of it from the time.


PHOTOCOPYING OF THIS PAGE IS RESTRICTED UNDER LAW.
ISBN: 9780170462419

# Whanganui War

20

**Historians follow hot-spots – places of action, danger and fighting. Conflict now flares in Whanganui and so there are new developments to unravel.**

The New Zealand Company says it has bought land on the banks of lower Whanganui River. Settlers begin arriving in February 1841. Lower-river Māori from Pūtiki pā generally see the new settlement as *their* town. Upper-river Māori generally oppose Pākehā settlement on the river. The Land Commissioner rules against the Company but says that most settlers bought land from it in good faith. He tells the Company to pay Māori compensation. Rangatira at Pūtiki tell settlers in early 1845 that the original land purchase will be honoured. When Te Mamaku comes back to the upper Whanganui River in late September 1846 he tells settlers he will protect them provided no soldiers are stationed there. The British then build a stockade and blockhouses and by early 1847 Whanganui has many soldiers in town.

*Whanganui.*

British artist John Gilfillan, his wife and their six children have settled in the Whanganui area. On the evening of 18 April 1847, six upriver Māori attack the Gilfillan farm. John escapes and heads for town, four hours away on foot. He thinks he is the target and his family will be safe. When he returns next morning with an armed party his wife is dead, three children are dead and another child badly wounded. Is it utu for a few days earlier when a young upriver Māori is accidentally shot in the face by a naval cadet and treated by a surgeon?

Te Mamaku's men capture five of the six upriver Māori attackers. A military court sentences four to death and hangs them at the stockade. The fifth is spared because of his age – he may have been 12 – and is banished from the region for life. Te Mamaku thinks the Māori should have had iwi justice, not British. He comes downriver to the outskirts of Whanganui in May with maybe 700 fighters to blockade it. Many settlers take refuge in town. On 19 May Te Mamaku attacks. His warriors burn and loot homes of outlying settlers and take stock. The Governor sends in reinforcements. By June, 800 British soldiers protect the 200 settlers and Māori at Pūtiki. The blockade ends when soldiers move out of the stockade and fight Te Mamaku. Two soldiers killed, 11 wounded; Māori have similar numbers. A truce is called. Te Mamaku goes back upriver.

*Pūtiki pā.*

## Mahi Skills

1 **Local history:** One of the men captured and sentenced to a convict settlement is Hōhepa Te Umuroa of Ngāti Hau. He took part in the attack on Boulcott's farm. He dies at the convict settlement. This makes authorities ask if the court martial and transportation is legal. The remaining prisoners of the group are released. Te Umuroa has to wait until 1988 when six elders of his iwi go to Tasmania and bring his remains home to be reburied by the Whanganui River. Explain what this says about long-term effects.

2 **Legal age:** Imagine an invading army is trying to take over New Zealand. State what age you think Government should require people wanting to enlist to be and give reasons for your answer.

3 **Actions:** State to whom these actions belong: *seek safety in town, accidentally shoots, makes land claims, passes a death sentence, escapes and runs for help, surrounds a town to isolate it, oppose Pākehā settlement, build military fortifications in town.*

4 **Predicting:** John Gilfillan is known as a gifted artist whose work gives historians a good idea of what New Zealand is like in the early days of colonisation. Think about his 1847 experience in Whanganui and work out what he may have done next. Research to see if you are correct and then collect two of his images to add to your work.

5 **Historians' responsibility:** John Gilfillan painted these images of Whanganui (page 61 and 62). Explain why historians should know a bit about the artists of paintings.


PHOTOCOPYING OF THIS PAGE IS RESTRICTED UNDER LAW.
ISBN: 9780170462419

# Kīngitanga 21

**Historians research people, attitudes and experiences to show how tension can build. Wiremu Tāmihana, sometimes called King Maker for his involvement with setting up a Māori King although he is one of several who do so, says he is left waiting at the Government's Native Office in Auckland for two days. He tells a missionary that he thinks Māori get treated like dogs.**

Disputes between Māori and Māori, and between Māori and Pākehā, continue. There are some near misses. One day in April 1851 some Hauraki Ngāti Paoa visit Auckland and scuffle with police when, it is said, a Ngāti Paoa policeman hits a chief. In Hauraki, Ngāti Paoa gather a force and set off for Auckland in waka. The Governor is warned and waits at Mechanics Bay with troops and a frigate. After negotiation, Ngāti Paoa are given tobacco and leave. Later they give the Governor a greenstone mere.

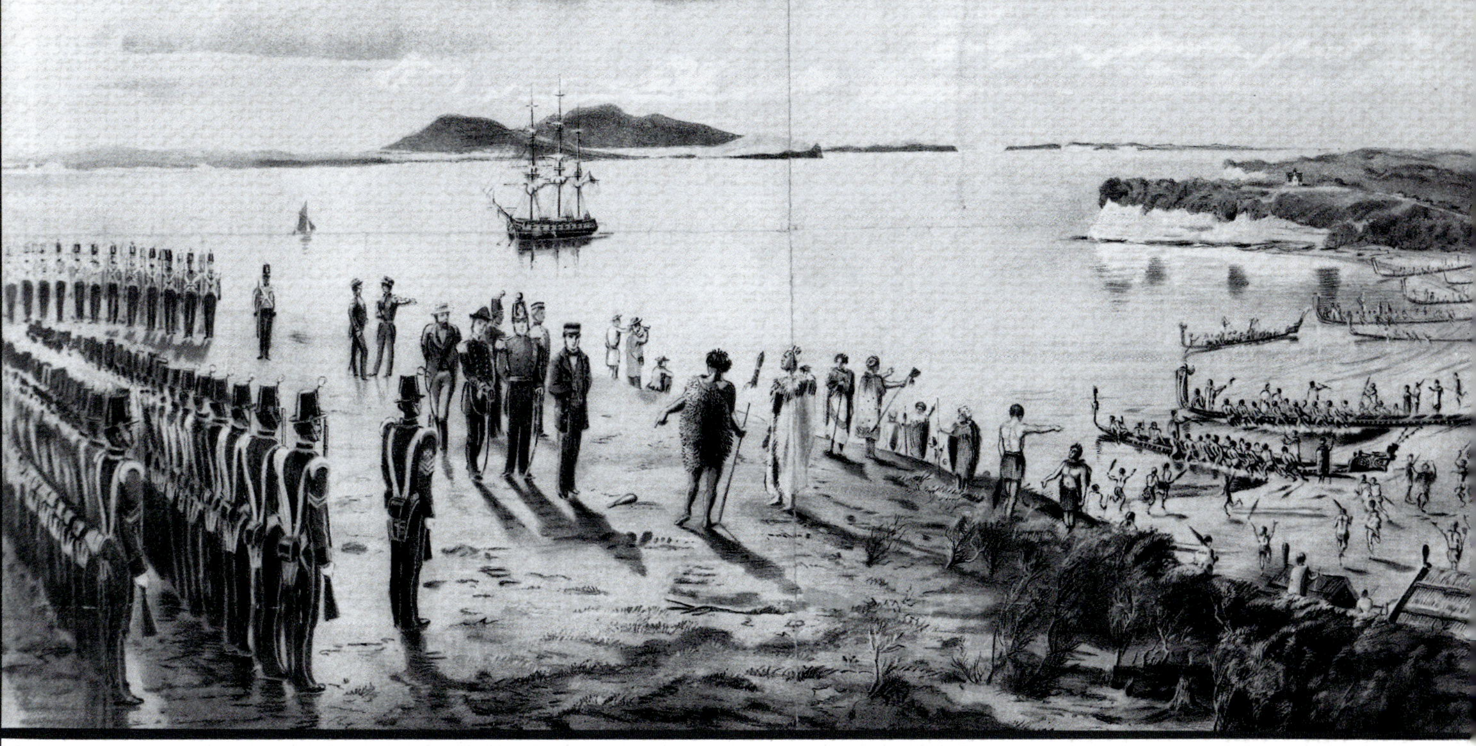

In New Plymouth people are nervous. In the 1820s many Te Āti Awa move south and now rangatira Wiremu Kīngi Te Rangitāke, who has traditional land at Waitara, has led nearly 600 people back to Taranaki. Some are in waka. Some drive stock up the coastline. The Governor does not welcome them. He threatens to destroy their waka. He tries to get them to settle on the north bank of Waitara River although the rohe of many hapū goes south of the river. Te Āti Awa settle on ancestral lands on the south bank. Kīngi is in a complex of three pā. But a few locals including Rawiri Waiaua are willing to sell land. Kīngi, on the side of Government in the Wellington war, is against selling Taranaki land. He writes to the Governor. Waitara shall not be given up, he says. Māori have done a lot of work on settler farms. I want friendly relations with settlers but should not have to sell land to get that. Settlers talk of Māori willing to sell land as friendlies, and Māori who are not as the anti-land-selling league. In August 1854 Māori under the order of rangatira Te Waitere Katatore kill Rawiri Waiaua, his brother and three others in a dispute over a block of land Rawiri wants to sell. A settler says Rawiri Waiaua, badly wounded, asks him to hide Rawiri's mere. He hides it in a mattress and Katatore and his men cannot find it. The settler later gives the mere to Rawiri's son. Government officials say they will not get involved as it is a 'quarrel between natives.' There is more fighting and killing. A Ngāti Ruanui man is killed for allegedly having an affair with the wife of an ally of Rawiri. Katatore is ambushed and killed. Settlers, hemmed in on a strip of coastal land at New Plymouth, keep pushing to buy land. And by now three other big events have happened.

Firstly, New Zealand's first parliament meets in 1854. Only men who own property can vote. This means Māori cannot vote as they have communal rights to land. Most MPs think they must look after settlers who elect them, that the Colonial Office will expect New Zealand to start paying the bills and one way will be to get Māori land. Secondly, settler numbers match those of Māori in 1858 and from then on pass them. Thirdly, there is now a Māori King and a King movement called Kīngitanga. The King is Te Wherowhero who takes the name Pōtatau, the Waikato chief who has been helping protect Auckland at the request of the Governor. He has mana with Māori and Pākehā and Governors, belongs to the chiefly line of Ngāti Mahuta, has been a great warrior, is kin with many iwi. Waikato is resource-rich in a good location, has Taupiri mountain and Waikato River, will be a good host. Rather than all Māori joining to become one united group, Kīngitanga sees a boundary can separate King's authority from Crown authority. The King says Kīngitanga is not against Pākehā settlement or the Queen or Crown sovereignty on Crown land. It wants to manage Māori affairs as Parliament manages settler affairs. It has its own stamps, rūnanga assemblies, magistrates, newspaper, Minister for Pākehā Affairs.

Some settlers think it is a good way to bring law to Māori areas, some a challenge to the Crown, some as part of the anti-land-selling league. Governors George Grey and Thomas Gore Brown see it as treason and a challenge to Crown authority and British settlement. Governor Grey cancels a plan of the previous Governor to hold a big hui for Māori rangatira. It would be unwise, he says, *to call a number of semi-barbarous Natives together to frame a Constitution for themselves.* Some North Island chiefs put lands at Pōtatau's feet but many important iwi such as Ngāpuhi, Te Arawa and Ngāti Porou do not join.

*Pōtatau Te Wherowhero.*


PHOTOCOPYING OF THIS PAGE IS RESTRICTED UNDER LAW.
ISBN: 9780170462419

Taranaki.

## Mahi Skills

1 **Local history:** Both Te Ātiawa and Te Āti Awa are used. Describe how you would go about finding if one version is more acceptable to them.

2 **Identifying changes:** Identify how Kīngitanga shows a changing relationship between Māori and Crown.

3 **Interpreting action:** Describe a time when a person may have expected to be treated differently to how he is.

4 **Attitudes (ways of thinking and feeling about something):** Explain an attitude of the following: Wiremu Kīngi, Te Waitere Katatore, Ngāti Paoa, the Colonial Office, Pōtatau Te Wherowhero, Kīngitanga, Governor Grey, Ngāti Porou, Ngāpuhi, Wiremu Tāmihana, Native Office, Rawiri Waiaua, settlers, MPs.

5 **Probability:** The wars are still going when Māori in 1867 are given four seats in Parliament. There are 72 Pākehā MPs then. Work out the probability of this helping the Māori war effort. Explain your reasoning.

# 22 Taranaki

**Historians look at tricky situations. Governor Browne has taken over from George Grey. He has to try to keep a balance between settlers wanting to buy land and Māori not wanting to sell it. So while he tries to make sure Māori keep land and get schools and hospitals, he also buys land. A tricky situation.**

Taranaki's Waitara is not for sale. Or is it? Young Te Āti Awa rangatira Teira offers to sell land there. In March 1859 Governor Gore Browne is in New Plymouth, which is becoming an armed camp, to talk to Māori about iwi feuds. Wiremu Kīngi Te Rangitāke says Government should not buy the land. Government buys the land. In January 1860 it decides to survey it. Kīngi writes to Browne. I want peace and friendship, he says. Why can we not meet to sort this out? On 4 March Browne orders soldiers to occupy the land. They build a camp of tents. They force Kīngi's people out. They tell Kīngi, Destroy new pā you have built on this land. If you don't, the blood of your people will be on your head. On 13 March a survey begins.

*Assault on Kaipopo pā.*

On 15 March Kīngi builds a fighting pā at Te Kohia at the end of the disputed land. The pā is small but hard to surround and in plain view of Camp Waitara. On 16 March Māori pull up survey pegs. Settlers begin to shift in to New Plymouth. On 17 March the Governor orders Kīngi and his men to surrender. They refuse. Soldiers open fire on the pā and keep firing all day. That night Māori abandon the pā. Māori begin to loot farms and kill settlers. Soldiers leave Camp Waitara and set up around town. Several hundred warriors from other iwi come to support Kīngi. On a hill at Waireka, they build Kaipopo pā out of fence posts, saplings and wire, and surround it with rifle pits.


PHOTOCOPYING OF THIS PAGE IS RESTRICTED UNDER LAW.
ISBN: 9780170462419

*1861 painting called* Māori driving off settlers' cattle *is controversial as some say brilliant and some say suggests Māori thievery.*

On 28 March the battle of Waireka begins. Generally it is thought that at 1 pm a British force of troops and local volunteers and militia set off to rescue settlers said to be trapped behind Māori near Waireka Stream. Warriors in Kaipopo pā notice them as they march along the beach. Warriors move out of the pā and take up position near the stream. The two groups start shooting at each other. By late afternoon, both are low on ammunition. Some British troops have been sent back to defend the town but all troops are under orders to be back by dark to defend it. About 5.30pm, troops march off and leave volunteers and militia to keep fighting. On the march, they pass by the captain and sailors from a warship that has landed. Sailors go to Kaipopo pā and capture it. Then they march back to town. Numbers killed at Kaipopo range from claims of 70 to 150 Māori, to one historian saying only one elderly Māori was there. The British claim a victory. A church minister says settlers did not need rescuing as they were sheltering at church property. On the morning of 27 June, soldiers at Camp Waitara see Te Āti Awa at their twin pā of Puketakauere and Onukukaitara on low hills and go to Puketakauere. No more than 200 men are in the pā. Another 150 lie in Onukukaitara rifle pits and in gullies. Soldiers bombard the pā, then invade. Hidden Māori cut them down. Local militia attacking from the rear get bogged down in swamp. About 30 soldiers dead, 34 wounded; it is thought Māori casualties are few but British report them as 130–150.

Now follow actions including evacuating settlers to Nelson and Auckland, building redoubts, sapping, destroying kāinga and pā; and burning of settler farms, killing of settlers, driving settlers' stock away, storming redoubts. Settlers are frightened, about 120 people die of disease in town, soldiers are embarrassed and Te Āti Awa warriors go home to plant crops. On 18 March 1861 there is a ceasefire that settles little although for a while Taranaki is peaceful. But Māori are still unhappy over the sale of land at Waitara, and Government delays sorting the land issue, something it has promised to do.

*Militia and volunteers at Jury's farmhouse in battle of Waireka.*

Waitara sets some Pākehā against Pākehā. Missionary Octavius Hadfield knows Kīngi. He thinks Governor Browne's actions are wrong. He tries to get officials to listen to him – letters, reports and petitions to newspapers, authorities in New Zealand and Britain, to Governor and Queen, to the Church Missionary Society whom he tells there has been a wicked attempt to bring about war. Parliament summons him and quizzes him for four hours. Some clergy support him. A former Chief Justice agrees with him. Some MPs support Kīngi's position. A bishop's wife says, How can the natives expect justice when people who covet every inch of their land are the makers of laws?

## Mahi Skills

1 **Local history:** The only people who can properly say what the Waitara area means to them are the locals. Explain why.

2 **Evaluating:** Evaluating means to draw conclusions from evidence. Evaluate how Governor Browne's balancing act works out.

3 **Supporting evidence:** Give evidence in support of the following ideas.
War may break out again in Taranaki. Not all Pākehā support the Government military actions.

4 **Assessing value of evidence:** State how much the image on page 67 helps you understand the situation in Taranaki at this time. Then explain what skills you use to help you make your statement. Use the word 'perspectives' in your explanation.

5 **Referencing:** State to what these refer and how. *Teira, Waitara, Waireka, Kaipopo, Onukukaitara, Octavius.*


PHOTOCOPYING OF THIS PAGE IS RESTRICTED UNDER LAW.
ISBN: 9780170462419

# Great South Road 23

**Historians identify groups. Even if they have records, they often cannot identify every person involved in an action. Queen's Redoubt has room for 450 troops. How much space would it take to write their names here? Calling them soldiers identifies them as a group of Crown forces.**

In the 1840s Auckland has raupō whare, tents, rough buildings, pot-holed tracks, cleared hills, surrounding fern and scrub. When war in the north breaks out, rumours start that Tainui tribes to the south have been asked to help Māori attack Auckland. Nightmares for settlers. Government wants its second capital to survive. It builds Fort Britomart (named after a ship) at Te Rerenga Ora Iti headland. It brings retired soldiers, named Fencibles, from Britain and sets them up in villages – Howick, Panmure, Onehunga, Ōtāhuhu. It gets protection from Te Wherowhero and his Tainui men who are set up at Māngere.

*Building the Great South Road, 1863.*

Down in Waikato Māori keep working hard on the land. The Governor gives them loans to buy ploughs, mills, vessels. Māori traders take waka laden with vegetables and fish up to Auckland and help keep settlers alive. They move goods for settlers and farmers, earn money and mana. *Ko Te Karere o Nui Tireni* is the first Government-sponsored newspaper for Māori. Tradesmen, including shipping agents, shipbuilders, millers and engineers, advertise in newspapers. Māori have their own trading bank. This wealthy and fertile Waikato is a magnet to settlers wanting land.

Until Kīngitanga arrives, Governors consult Te Wherowhero on matters concerning Māori. But in the late 1850s Te Wherowhero is Māori King. He is getting pushed into being out of step with Government. Some Kīngitanga warriors have already fought Government, in Taranaki. After the Taranaki War, the Māori King asks the Governor to keep Pākehā to the north of Mangatāwhiri Stream. Waikato Māori will stay south. The two sides can trade with each other. But no settlers are to go on to Māori land. Although there is not yet an area called the King Country, the Mangatāwhiri Stream is an aukati – a line not to be crossed.

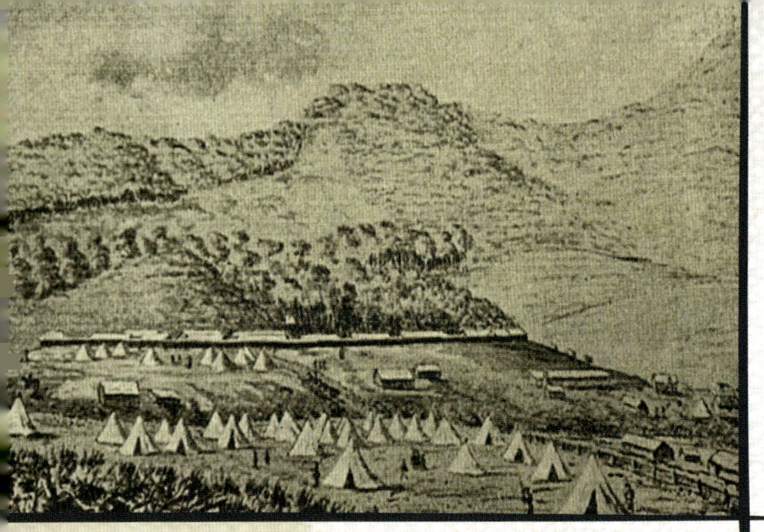

Queen's Redoubt.

Governor George Grey wants to get rid of Kīngitanga resistance. When Te Wherowhero dies in 1860 Grey warns that getting another king will be seen as an act of defiance towards the Crown. Te Wherowhero's son Tāwhiao becomes the new King. He pledges peace. Grey says, I will dig around Kīngitanga until it falls. Then the great Waikato land can open for Pākehā settlement. He tells Britain, Auckland is in danger of Māori attack. He gets it to send more soldiers out. But how will he get soldiers, artillery and supplies from Auckland to Waikato? Māori have waka and shipping on the Waikato River. There are dirt tracks, fit only for dry weather, that go to outlying settlements. After that, hills, swamps, bush, forest. Governor Grey orders a road to be built – the Great South Road. From January 1862 General Cameron's army spend 18 months building the road. Every available soldier clears bush and chops down trees. On average, 1700 men work on it each day. They build redoubts along it. In March 1862 Governor Grey writes to Cameron. Build a post near Mangatāwhiri Stream for soldiers, he says. Cameron decides to put it near the Ngāti Tamaoho village of Pokino (today's Pōkeno) which is by the stream. It is believed Pokino has been occupied since settlement began in Aotearoa. Soldiers destroy Pokino; it may have been abandoned. They take all its supplies. They build Queen's Redoubt. It has a parade area, guardrooms, officers' quarters, stores, hospital and library. They put up a telegraph line on kauri poles from Auckland to the redoubt. On 11 July General Cameron shifts into his new headquarters.

## Mahi Skills

1 **Local history:** In May of 1844 Māori host a week-long hākari (feast) at Remuera, attended by several thousand Māori and Pākehā. They put up a huge shed and tents, provide vast amounts of potatoes, sharks, pigs, tea, tobacco, sugar. The Governor visits one day and Māori haka, armed with guns and tomahawks. Grand occasions like this make history. Find out if any grand occasions happened in your area.

2 **Following direction:** Either download or draw a sketch map of the location of the following which go in a fairly straight line and in order of north to south, in the early 1860s. *Auckland, Great South Road, Mangatāwhiri Stream, Meremere, Rangiriri, Ngāruawāhia, Rangiaowhia, Ōrākau, the area that will be known as King Country.*

3 **Identifying groups:** Name as many different groups as you can from this chapter. What will you call the group who feasted in 1844 (see Mahi 1 above)?

4 **Discerning change:** In 1844 the *Southern Cross* newspaper says, *The present European population ... would have been literally starved out of the country but for the extraordinary exertions made by the aboriginal inhabitants to supply them with cheap provisions. Māori,* it says, *are the greatest benefit and the greatest blessing we have in New Zealand.* Down the track, the newspaper will say *Tainui tribes have to be attacked and their lands stripped from them.* Explain the change in attitude.

5 **Interpreting decisions:** Describe Government actions that might be seen as helping set Crown and Kīngitanga on a collision course.


PHOTOCOPYING OF THIS PAGE IS RESTRICTED UNDER LAW.
ISBN: 9780170462419

# Waikato 24

**Historians are good at summarising – choosing the most important facts. Otherwise just one event, such as the attack on a Pukekohe church, might take up a whole book or a whole day to talk about. Nothing wrong with spending days talking about an event; some historians say it is the best way to tell history. But when you have limited time and space, being able to summarise is a useful skill.**

Albert Barracks in Auckland.

In Auckland, Pākehā men aged 16 to 55 are required for military service. But no lunatics, MPs, or priests. Other men volunteer. Town Māori get a night curfew. On 9 July 1863 Governor Grey issues a notice. Waikato Māori living in the Government-controlled area south of Auckland must swear allegiance to the British Queen or go to Waikato. Magistrates enter Māori villages. Many Māori have ties with Waikato. Swear loyalty to the British Queen when her army is ready to invade Waikato? If they swear does it mean they will have to fight for the Crown against their relatives? Some leave in waka. Some go down the Great South Road.

On 11 July Governor Grey issues another notice. It says Māori have driven away Europeans living quietly on their own lands in Waikato, have plundered European property, taken wives and children, caused the murder of officers and soldiers at Taranaki, approved the murders, committed crimes elsewhere, rescued or sheltered criminals, are assembling in armed bands, are threatening to ravage Auckland and murder peaceable settlers, are offering safe passage through territories to armed parties, are unable or unwilling to prevent these evil acts.

Therefore, he says, he has to set up posts on the Waikato River to protect lives and property and stop armed and evil-disposed people from passing to rob and murder Europeans. And those who wage war against Her Majesty or remain in arms must understand they will forfeit the right to the possession of their lands guaranteed to them by the Treaty of Waitangi. How long would it take for Waikato to get that message? One magistrate suggests it does not reach Waikato until 15 July.

*Pukekohe church battle.*

On 12 July the Queen's Redoubt soldiers march out to put up military posts on Waikato River. They cross the Mangatāwhiri Stream and set up camp on an old hill pā site. On 17 July Cameron sees Māori on Koheroa ridge and leads a force to chase them. They kill about fifteen. Skirmishing goes on for weeks. Māori cross the Waikato River in waka, make smokeless camps in forest on both sides of Great South Road, ambush carts and wagonloads of soldiers and supplies, raid settler clearings, take cattle, kill settlers. Soldiers build redoubts. Those at Queen's Redoubt sleep in their clothes and watch for Māori hiding in the bush.

Some young people are involved. At Pukekohe, an isolated farming settlement south of Auckland, an armed volunteer company use the church as a garrison. About 17 men and a boy of maybe 14 are there one morning doing chores such as cleaning rifles. Suddenly a Māori war party charges out of the bush. Volunteers say later it has 300–400 warriors; a Māori says 200. For several hours the groups shoot at each other. Māori remove their dead and wounded under heavy fire. Their snipers shoot from up a pūriri tree and on a house roof. About 1 pm soldiers begin to arrive and at about 4 pm British bugles in the bush sound for 150 soldiers coming in. After an hour, fighting ends with defenders having three killed or mortally wounded and eight wounded; Māori are said to have lost more than forty. They take most away but have to hide some bodies in tree hollows. The Pākehā boy is said to have been brave, carrying ammo from the church to shooters. Today the church still has bullet holes in its walls.

Māori have defensive lines against General Cameron's forces. The first is Meremere – a big gunfighter pā overlooking Waikato River and manned at its peak by maybe a thousand under Wiremu Tāmihana. All Kīngitanga iwi have warriors there. Cameron's armoured river fleet gets ready to carry men and supplies on the river. His troops force Māori at Te Teoteo to withdraw south; troops build a redoubt and drag up an Armstrong gun. On 30 October they shell Meremere. A trader is said to have given Māori three ship guns and they have hauled them from Raglan and brought them by waka to Meremere. But they have no shells and though they make some from things like iron chain and nails, they cannot stop the British fleet sailing past Meremere and landing upriver. Soldiers storm Meremere pā. Nobody there. Soldiers pitch tents on the hill, put up their flag and build a redoubt.

*Waikato River gunboat Pioneer, New Zealand's first purpose-built warship.*



PHOTOCOPYING OF THIS PAGE IS RESTRICTED UNDER LAW. ISBN: 9780170462419

The second defence is Rangiriri. After leaving Meremere, Māori men, women and children work quickly on Rangiriri. Important Māori chiefs including King Tāwhiao and Wiremu Tāmihana are there, but the pā has only maybe about 500 men, and women to reload muskets. On 20 November a British force with artillery attack the still unfinished pā. The river fleet takes more troops upstream. Soldiers followed by a naval force go ashore and charge the pā. They chase and shoot defenders. But when they attack rifle pits they have to take cover. Their ladders do not reach high enough up the banks and Māori fire down on them. In the night, most defenders slip away. Soldiers discard their planned dawn attack when remaining Māori raise a white flag. People still debate the meaning of that flag. Surrender or a wish to talk terms? Casualties are said to be 35–47 British dead and maybe 85 wounded, and 50 Māori dead.

Cameron tells Kīngitanga, Peace talk has to come from the Governor. Governor Grey says, Māori must leave Ngāruawāhia before I will come to talk. King Tāwhiao goes south into Ngāti Maniapoto territory. The Governor does not come. Soldiers go into Ngāruawāhia. They put up the Union Jack and General Cameron makes it his base. The third line of defence is the Pāterangi line. Pāterangi pā and others are on low ridges between Te Awamutu and Waipā River. Māori begin work on the line after Rangiriri. Warriors from a dozen iwi are there. Still not enough to both man the pā and send raids on soldiers. They need more food, water, weapons. On 28 January, soldiers march from camps and by lunchtime next day they see Pāterangi. Another piece of engineering to admire. For three weeks they shell and shoot Pāterangi. Māori hang on. They say soldiers' shooting is maumau paura – a waste of gunpowder. On 11 February at Waiāri on a hot afternoon, soldiers are bathing in Mangapiko Stream. Māori hide in fern on the opposite bank. They open fire. Six soldiers are killed, eight wounded. Reports of Māori casualties vary from 20 to 40 deaths. Two wounded Māori are taken prisoner.

*Rangiriri.*

## Mahi Skills

1 **Local history:** Stories tell of sadness of Auckland Māori at leaving their houses and gardens, knowing soldiers will come to their ancient villages. Make notes on how movement affects people and places.

2 **Framing questions:** Make questions for which the following are answers. *Curfew, Lunatic, Kinship ties, Meremere, Rangiriri, Waiāri, Swear allegiance, Magistrate, Maumau paura, Governor Grey.*

3 **Analysis of a construction:** One thing people agree on is how good Rangiriri and Pāterangi pā are. Find a plan of one and comment on it.

4 **Summary:** Make a summary of two of the following. *Grey's second notice, Pukekohe church battle, Waiāri fight, the three defensive lines.*

5 **Prioritising:** Make a list of ten words from this chapter you think it would be respectful for people to spell correctly.

ISBN: 9780170462419 PHOTOCOPYING OF THIS PAGE IS RESTRICTED UNDER LAW. 

# 25 Rangiaowhia

Historians try to be respectful. They know they are talking of people who are no longer able to speak for themselves. Some people criticise historians for concentrating on sensational events which are still hurtful for ancestors. Some see Rangiaowhia as an example of that.

Nine days after Waiāri. It is night-time. General Cameron gives an order. Two part-Māori guides lead troops followed by a supply column along a bush track. They pass close to Pāterangi pā. They move silently and swiftly. No bugles. Swords and bridle chains of Colonel Marmaduke Nixon's cavalry are muffled with cloth. They go along the bank of Mangaohoi Stream lined with swamps and forest. They manage to pass without alerting sentries. At dawn next day they reach Te Awamutu. In the morning they suddenly appear in front of the Māori settlement of Rangiaowhia. Cavalry dismount. They and foot-soldiers attack Rangiaowhia. It is Sunday, 21 February 1864.

Today Rangiaowhia is used with the word controversial – something that causes disagreement. It is still debated and discussed by historians and descendants of Ngāti Apakura. There are many accounts and often they contradict each other. One accepted fact is that it still causes pain today in Māori descendants. Some call it a day of terrorism, others a massacre. Crown soldiers who are obeying orders say they are fighting to end what they think is Māori rebellion. They have learned that if they can it is a good move to go round pā such as the Pāterangi line rather than attack front-on. Rangiaowhia has food supplies for Māori. Attacking it will damage Māori economically and emotionally as well as politically.

*Rangiaowhia.*

In 1864 Rangiaowhia is about two miles long with about 700 people. It has orchards, Anglican and Catholic churches (whare karakia) and mission schools, a dam, flour mill, whare, blacksmith, fences, roads, bridges, cows, pigs, wheat, maize, fowls, potatoes, oats. The men of Rangiaowhia are at Pāterangi when soldiers arrive. Nobody knows how many people are left in the village. A number often given is about 200. It is said Māori tell Bishop Selwyn that women, children and elderly are taking refuge at unfortified and undefended Rangiaowhia and ask him to tell General Cameron and so Kīngitanga understand people in Rangiaowhia will be unharmed.

Now they scatter. Into a church, into whare. Some accounts say soldiers are ordered to leave the church alone. Sergeant McHale, a cavalryman, is shot and killed when he fires into a whare. So is another soldier. Soldiers surround the whare and open fire. Those inside shoot Marmaduke Nixon and another trooper trying to rescue McHale's body. Soldiers kill Māori who try to surrender or escape. The whare catches on fire; some witnesses say it is an accident, maybe from muskets. Others say soldiers deliberately set it on fire. An elderly man comes out with his hands up. Soldiers shoot him. Are the others inside too scared now to come out? They are incinerated. Other whare burn. Accidentally or set on fire? One story is that a woman is at the local puna with tamariki getting them ready for church. She keeps them safe by getting them to use reeds to help them breathe as they hide under the water.

Descendants have stories of deliberate fires, killing of elderly and women and children, rape, soldiers shooting people having prayers in a whare karakia and soldiers setting whare on fire when people refuse to come out. Another story says that when soldiers reach the village they see *natives in all directions* who open fire on them. Official British records state 12 Māori dead, including two chiefs, 12 wounded, 33 taken prisoner including 21 women and children. Five British soldiers are dead. Some official military sources make no reference to the killing of women or children. Some unofficial estimates say more than 100 Māori die.

Soldiers hold Rangiaowhia for a few hours. Then Cameron orders them back to Te Awamutu. A report says a *little booty was secured as loot* and when troops go back a few days later they take *an exceedingly large number of pigs, poultry, rabbits, vegetables, ... mats, tomahawks, greenstones, guns, cooking utensils, clothing, cartouche boxes, scarcely a soldier returning without some trophy of victory.*

## Mahi Skills

1. **Local history:** Explain how respect for people involved in events means historians understand that written and oral accounts may differ, that knowledge resides with iwi and hapū, that families of soldiers are also affected and may hold histories.
2. **Perspectives in sources:** The original painter of the image on page 74 is John Wilson who fights at Pāterangi, Hairini and Rangiaowhia. It is called *The Fight at Rangiao(w)hia for the Recovery of McHale's Body* and it shows the fall of Colonel Nixon top second from left, Captain Thomas McDonnell running to help Nixon and Cameron and his staff at right. Suggest reasons he chose that perspective and how a Māori perspective might be different.
3. **War terminology:** Some people say Rangiaowhia Māori deaths are casualties of war and some say they are victims of kōhuru (murder). Explain the difference.
4. **Applying a proverb:** *Nā tō rourou, nā taku rourou ka ora ai te iwi* (With your food basket and my food basket, the people will thrive). Apply this to Rangiaowhia before 1864.
5. **Understanding controversy:** Provide examples of why Rangiaowhia is controversial today.

# 26 Ōrākau

**Historians know that wars have some standout events. It may be they capture popular imagination or are more controversial than others, or test historians' skills when they have to assess the value of available evidence. Rangiaowhia is one of those events. So is Ōrākau.**

Rewi Maniapoto moves warriors to Hairini ridge, between Te Awamutu and Rangiaowhia. He is still fortifying when a Crown force with two Armstrong guns marches from Te Awamutu on 22 February 1864. Soldiers discharge several rounds. A storming party advances. Many Māori get away through swamp. It is said about 20 die and three British die but numbers are disputed.

Kihikihi is a Ngāti Maniapoto kāinga. No natural or man-made defences, another supplier of food for Māori. On 23 February British troops arrive. Unable to defend the kāinga, Rewi Maniapoto and his people cross the Puniu River. They can see soldiers destroy the kāinga, burn the Hui Te Rangiora meeting house and cart away produce and livestock. In March Tūhoe and Ngāti Raukawa fighters arrive. Give us Ōrākau to use our guns and ammunition, they say. They have been too heavy to carry all this way for nothing. I don't want to fight at Ōrākau, says Rewi. Peach trees but no water supply. Soldiers will surround it easily. But he finally agrees and they build a pā. Crown forces march overnight, and attack at dawn on 31 March. There are five attacks over three days. To face a force of about 1400, Rewi has about 300, many of them women and children. Hine-i-tūrama Ngātiki of Ngāti Whakaue, wife of Phillip Tapsell, is visiting her daughter in Waikato. She and daughter help defend Ōrākau. Both die and are buried there.

Rangatira Hitiri Te Paerata of Ngāti Raukawa is an eyewitness. He says Rangiaowhia, where he was, makes his father lead Raukawa into war. When soldiers give up trying to take Ōrākau by assault, he says, they surround it. Māori have no water and only raw potatoes but are helped by the recital of brave acts of ancestors whose motto is *Me mate te tangata, me mate mo te whenua* – the warrior's death is to die for the land. Ōrākau people are not frightened, he says, because their hearts are filled with fury. The defenders run out of bullets so they fire peach-stones and wood plugs. Around noon on the third day soldiers get close to the pā. They throw hand grenades. Māori manage to pick some up before they explode and throw them back. Major Mair appears and all defender guns aim at him. Stop fighting, he says. You are surrounded. If you keep on, you will be killed and your women and children will die with you.

Ahumai, sister to Hitiri Te Paerata, says, *Ki te mate ngā tāne, me mate anō ngā wāhine me ngā tamariki*. If the men die, the women and children must die also. Hitiri Te Paerata's father and Hapurona and Rewi say, *Ake ake ake e hoa, ka whawhai tonu mātou!* Friend, we will fight on forever, forever and forever! The people repeat these words. But soon the situation is so bad that the defenders form up in a body with females in the middle. They put their last bullets in the guns and leave the pā.


PHOTOCOPYING OF THIS PAGE IS RESTRICTED UNDER LAW.
ISBN: 9780170462419

Cavalry and Forest Rangers chase and shoot. Hitiri Te Paerata's father, brothers and uncle are killed. Sister Ahumai is shot through a shoulder, her waist, and has a thumb shot away. Hitiri Te Paerata says he hears that Major Mair goes in to look after wounded, and tries to stop soldiers killing Hine-i-tūrama. Maybe, he says, soldiers don't know she is a woman and are enraged at the death of their officer. Mair carries her to a corner and runs off to help another woman but soldiers kill Hine-i-tūrama. Hitiri Te Paerata says he mentions Mair to show some Europeans are kind to them. He says when wounded cry for water he runs to the swamp with a calabash. Soldiers let him pass without firing. Some Māori, including Rewi Maniapoto, escape and go south. Estimates are at least 160 Māori and 17 soldiers are dead, many wounded. Kīngitanga lives now in Ngāti Maniapoto land south of the Puniu River. This boundary is something generally accepted rather than a set aukati.

And Ahumai? She survives and a story is that a year later, her iwi have a new religion called Pai Mārire and are at a kāinga near Ōruanui. A young Pākehā naval officer and his Māori guide arrive. The tohunga decides the Pākehā will be a sacrifice in their religious ceremony. Ahumai is said to walk across the marae and sit in front of him. She has mana. She still has scars from Ōrākau. Her action saves the Pākehā's life.

## Mahi Skills

1. **Local history:** Suggest ways locals may have knowledge of Ōrākau and details not in written accounts and which may contradict written accounts. Some historians, for example, attribute the Māori response to Mair's message of surrender to Hauraki Tonganui, a Taupō chief.
2. **Locating a specific place:** Make a sketch map of Ōrākau's location. You might add distances, maybe in miles as they are in 1864.
3. **Delving:** Go deeply into the painting above by explaining the specific actions it shows and the causes and results of the actions.
4. **Researching:** *Rewi's Last Stand* is a 1925 silent movie remade as a talkie in 1940. Some people object to the name because it suggests Rewi gives up whereas he keeps resisting with different methods. Research other ways Ōrākau is remembered.
5. **Making a narrative:** Explain causes and effects of Ōrākau, including why Pākehā now call an area The King Country.

# 27 Tauranga

**Historians look at how groups make and follow rules. At a pā on Wairoa River in Tauranga, Hēnare Taratoa writes down a code of conduct for warriors to follow while they fight Crown forces. It is in a letter dated 28 March 1864 addressed to Colonel Greer. Māori remember this code during the battles of Gate Pā and Te Ranga.**

Some Tauranga Māori send supplies and fighters to Kīngitanga in Waikato. Crown forces now focus on Tauranga. They ship in troops and close off the harbour. They have a big military camp with redoubts at Te Papa, site of today's Tauranga town.

Ngāi Te Rangi fighters come home from Waikato. Their leader is Rāwiri Puhirake. They want to get Crown forces to attack them at a place Māori choose. They rebuild an old pā and send a message. *Bring your soldiers to fight at this pā. We will even make a road for them.* No reply. Māori leaders gather at Pōterīwhi pā on Wairoa River. They prepare rules for fighting. Hēnare Taratoa is a former mission teacher. He writes the rules down as a code of conduct for how to behave. It says wounded or captured soldiers will be saved, unarmed soldiers will be handed over to the law, soldiers who flee to the house of a priest will be saved, unarmed Pākehā will be spared. They send a copy to the soldiers and another challenge to attack. No reply.

Gate Pā.

Several hundred Māori gather near Te Papa. Crown forces do not take the bait. Māori go to Pukehinahina, a small hill about two miles from Te Papa. They start building a pā. It is also known as Gate Pā, as a gate sits in the boundary between missionary and Māori land. Defenders are mostly Ngāi Te Rangi, supported by Ngāti Paoa and other Hauraki and Waikato warriors. They put their red war flag behind their actual position. It might trick enemy gunners into thinking the pā is further away so they fire long.


PHOTOCOPYING OF THIS PAGE IS RESTRICTED UNDER LAW.
ISBN: 9780170462419

On 21 April General Cameron arrives with more soldiers. On 26 April ships bring sailors and marines who unload artillery and take it to within firing distance of Gate Pā. This will be the heaviest bombardment of the wars, they say. It will blast the pā off the hill. Soldiers move out of Te Papa and station themselves around Gate Pā. In the dark, they creep over mudflats and hide behind the pā. It rains heavily all night. Nine British officers who are to lead the attack meet for dinner at the Mission House. Only one is going to survive next day.

On 29 April at first light gunners start bombarding. They keep going for many hours. In the rain guns turn earth to mud. At 4 pm there is no sign of life inside the pā. Defenders are hidden. Among them is Hēni Te Kiri Karamū, who refuses to leave her brother when women are ordered to go. She is he wahine toa – a female warrior. She supports Kīngitanga and fought in the Waikato wars.

*Hēnare Taratoa.*

Cameron gives the order to attack. The assault party forms up four abreast. The leader raises his sword and waves the men forward. Māori in the hidden trenches fire. Māori in the pā's two redoubts fire. Soldiers are confused. Most of their officers have been shot. Commander Hay is wounded and carried to safety. A surgeon dresses Hay's wounds under fire and goes to help others lying hurt in the pā. The front soldiers flee in panic. They leave dead and wounded. Cameron has to call off the attack. British have 30–35 dead and 75–80 wounded, about twice estimated Māori numbers. In the night Māori gather their wounded who can be moved, and collect muskets. They slip past Crown forces. They remember the code of conduct. They do not loot or mutilate. Hēni Te Kiri Karamū takes water to the dying Colonel Booth. Some historians say this action was done by Hēnare Taratoa or Te Ipu so maybe they also gave water to wounded soldiers. It is said that some Māori women take wounded soldiers home to look after them.

How could so few Māori beat so many Crown fighters? Some say, the assault party was cowardly and should be ashamed for leaving dead and dying behind. Some say, Māori fought an intelligent and brave battle. Cameron cops blame. Army and naval units blame each other. When the Auckland newspaper criticises naval forces, sailors march to its building and start pulling it down. The newspaper agrees to print the sailors' version of events. The Secretary of State for the Colonies writes to the Governor. We have given you 10,000 English troops, he says. You will not continue spending blood and money longer than is necessary to get a just and lasting peace.

A soldier who paints the images of Hēnare Taratoa and the pā after the battle is Horatio Robley. As a young British Army officer he arrives in Auckland in 1864 and comes down with his regiment to take part in the Tauranga war. His sketches, especially of dead and dying Māori warriors, are published in the *London Illustrated News*. They put a human face on what is happening and shock people into saying the wars should stop.

Māori start a pā at Te Ranga, three miles inland from Gate Pā. A scouting party finds them. Colonel Greer leads a force to attack the unfinished pā on 21 June. A lot of hand-to-hand fighting and Rāwiri Puhirake, hero of Gate Pā, is killed. So is Hēnare Taratoa. Māori pull back. Cavalry chase but cannot get through the bush. More than a hundred defenders are buried in trenches. It is said officers gather to pay respect to Rāwiri Puhirake as he is buried. Māori have 100–120 dead and 27 wounded; Crown forces have 13 dead and 39 wounded.

ISBN: 9780170462419
PHOTOCOPYING OF THIS PAGE IS RESTRICTED UNDER LAW.

*Morning after Battle of Gate Pā.*

A few days later Māori give up their weapons at Te Papa. In August a formal peacemaking includes land confiscation, land surveys and military settlers on the land. A new town of Tauranga begins. Some Māori go into the hills. Others belonging to Pai Mārire, a new religion, are there too. Ngāi Te Rangi rangatira Pene Taka Tuaia, engineer of Pukehinahina, is also there. Now there is utu for the death of his kin, Rāwiri Puhirake. Hill people skirmish with Crown forces. They make armed raids on camps, take away surveyors' theodolites. Major Mair and a troop of Te Arawa are called in. They burn kāinga, dig up and destroy vegetables, kill cattle and horses. Hill people shoot several militia and soldiers. Gradually the area calms.

## Mahi Skills

1 **Local history:** When Augustus Selwyn, chaplain to the troops, goes back to England he orders stained glass windows about the battle of Gate Pā for a chapel at Lichfield Cathedral. Explain how local history can morph into something that affects not just the local area.

2 **Planning a field trip:** Make notes you could use in a group discussion about a field trip to the Tauranga area to look at historical places.

3 **Recognising differences:** Show differences between Gate Pā and Te Ranga.

4 **Imagining:** Explain your reaction as a person in Britain seeing Robley's drawings of warriors.

5 **Understanding an individual:** Find out more about a person from this chapter. For example, starting points for Robley could be *Burmese black bear, romance with a rangatira's daughter, child he leaves behind, book about moko which some historians say helps save the art of moko, collection of mokomokai that earn him the name of head-hunter and of which many Māori and Pākehā including his own family disapprove, later effort to sell the collection to fund a return to New Zealand.*


PHOTOCOPYING OF THIS PAGE IS RESTRICTED UNDER LAW.
ISBN: 9780170462419

# Raupatu 28

**Historians look at how ideas and actions of people in the past impact on lives. Sometimes impact is long-term. An example is raupatu – confiscation of Māori land. It is so long-term that even though it happened in the 1860s, its impact continues today. Conditions at that time and place – the historical context – are helpful for historians to know. They do not use that knowledge to excuse actions, just to try to understand them.**

In 1863 Parliament passes an Act that says Government can confiscate land from iwi considered to have 'engaged in open rebellion against Her Majesty's authority'. Settlers will be able to take over this land. Several million acres of land are confiscated.

*Confiscations add to the numbers of people forced to leave their homes.*

A Government perspective on the wars is that Māori fighters are rebels who must be punished. New Zealand and British Governments are paying for the wars, which are expensive. Raupatu will punish Māori 'rebels' and help pay for the wars. A Māori perspective is that Māori are fighting to defend their lands. If I die, I die for the land, says one warrior. If you take the land, says another, where are we to live?

By the time confiscations start, Parliament has passed other Acts. The Public Works Land Act of 1864 lets Government take Māori land for public works, such as a road between Whanganui and New Plymouth. Some Māori land is taken instead of Pākehā land beside it because Government can pay owners less compensation, or none. Some roads are put through Māori reserves. Some land is taken for schools, no schools appear, land is not returned. Another lets Government take Māori land when chiefs do not give up fugitives hiding in their territories. Many settlers and newspapers say confiscation is good. One paper talks of bloodthirsty murderers in Waikato and says the only way to deal with them is by confiscation and sword. Some politicians disapprove. One MP says raupatu is an enormous crime, is against the Treaty of Waitangi and will drive every Māori into a state of hopeless rebellion. A former Commissioner of Crown Land supports it but says Government should take 'not one acre more' than is necessary for military settlements; he says it is immoral, and that confiscation and military settlement will lead to a war of extermination. A retired Chief Justice says that Ireland is an example of how little a country can be calmed down by confiscating land, how the claims of ex-owners are remembered down the generations, and how the brooding sense of wrong breaks out from time to time in fresh disturbance and crime. Not all politicians stay true to their view. The one who describes raupatu as an enormous crime becomes Native Minister and causes a huge amount of confiscation. Some groups in Britain say confiscation will make Natives fight with the madness of despair. The Secretary of State for the Colonies says the sense of injustice will turn Natives into a desperate banditti taking shelter in the interior from chasing police or military. Many soldiers, including General Cameron, are unhappy. Why should we fight a war to get land for New Zealand settlers? they ask.

Confiscation is often disorganised and confusing with many lost records and documents, and so many groups involved – Governor, Parliament, Colonial Office, military, land-buyers, speculators wanting to invest, Compensation Court which is supposed to compensate kūpapa and neutral Māori whose land has been confiscated, lawyers and court officials. The Crown returns some land although not always to the original holders. Later it reduces amounts of confiscations in some areas. By 1869 the Native Minister decides confiscations are nothing but an expensive mistake.

Iwi are affected in different ways. Land surrounding Rangiaowhia is confiscated. Local Ngāti Apakura become known as the landless people. Waikato land confiscation includes much of what is said to be the world's best farming land.

Ngāti Maniapoto who fight in the wars, largely avoids confiscation; Government thinks their land is hard to access and not valuable. Tūhoe's confiscated land includes their only big areas of flat lands with access to the coast. Physically, raupatu takes away the greatest Māori resource; economically, it damages their economy which is based on land; emotionally, it leaves feelings of injustice, despair, anger, confusion. Ngāti Mahuta chief Tāmati Ngāpora says, If the blood of our people only had been spilled and the land remained, then this trouble would have been over long ago. All Māori in confiscated areas get labelled tangata hara (rebels) even if their hapū did not fight. It helps cause new religions and war again in Taranaki.

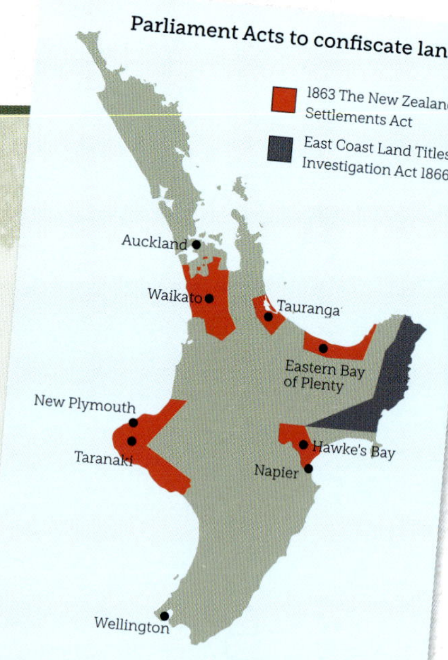


## Mahi Skills

1. **Local history:** While raupatu affects the North Island, the South Island has been affected by massive land-buying. Decide on six questions about confiscated and sold land you might try to find answers for in the local community. Start each question with one of Who, What, When, Where, Why, How.

2. **Historical context:** Describe the historical context of raupatu.

3. **Replicating:** Copy the map and write a paragraph about confiscation and why only the North Island is shown.

4. **Selecting a graph:** Explain what type of graph you would use to show the following data about Māori land-holding. Each set contains the year followed by acres held.

   1840 – 66 400 000 • 1852 – 34 000 000 • 1860 – 21 400 000
   1891 – 11 079 486 • 1911 – 7 137 205 • 1920 – 4 787 686 • 1939 – 4 028 903

5. **Methods of delivery:** As an expert in raupatu, explain which of these actions to show raupatu you would rather do and why. *Fronting podcasts, being a social influencer, creating graphics, drawing pictures, writing reports, filming.*


PHOTOCOPYING OF THIS PAGE IS RESTRICTED UNDER LAW.
ISBN: 9780170462419

# Buying Te Wai Pounamu

# 29

**Historians examine policies – courses of action adopted by organisations, such as the Crown buying land from Māori. Raupatu does not apply to Te Wai Pounamu but land is alienated another way – the buying and selling ideas introduced by Europeans.**

When Europeans arrive, Ngāi Tahu is the main iwi in Te Wai Pounamu (the South Island). Ngāi Tahu provides food to whaling ships and local chiefs allow some shore whalers to set up stations under rangatira authority. Some Māori women marry whalers. Then organised British immigration starts. Sell us your land, says the New Zealand Company, Crown, Governor, immigrants. And Māori end up selling about 34.5 million acres of land – more than half the land mass of New Zealand. Mana Māori takes a big hit.

Ngāi Tahu makes its first claim against the Crown for breach of contract in 1849. Only nine years after the Treaty of Waitangi is signed. How long do they wait for any closure? Until the 1990s. The organisation Government has set up to investigate such claims, the Waitangi Tribunal, says that in getting so *much* land and leaving Ngāi Tahu so *little* land, the Crown acts unconscionably and in repeated breach of the Treaty of Waitangi. It talks of 'grave injustices' based on 'unconscionable theft' by the Crown. 'Unconscionably' means shockingly bad and unfair; 'theft' means stealing.

How does it all go so wrong? Experts outline that process. Crown refuses to pay a fair price for land. Crown says it will set aside adequate reserves of about ten per cent of the acres sold. Crown does not. Crown promises to set up schools and hospitals. Crown does not. Crown alienates Māori from traditional mahinga kai – food and other resources, and places where they get those resources. Crown alienates Māori from other sacred places such as urupā burial sites. Deeds of sale have vague boundaries.

*Lyttelton is one of three towns planned for Canterbury colony.*

An example. The Canterbury Purchase, also known as the Kemp Deed. In Britain, Edward Gibbon Wakefield asks John Robert Godley to found a colony in New Zealand based on beliefs of the Church of England. Godley forms a Canterbury Association. Some powerful people support it – MPs, peers, Archbishop of Canterbury. The capital city of the colony is to be called Christ Church after the college Godley attended. Nothing so far to suggest any Māori-type organisation and governing; everything to suggest British-type organisation and governing.

In New Zealand, Governor Grey sends Land Commissioner Henry Kemp off to buy land. In June 1848 Henry is on a ship in Akaroa Harbour. So are a group of Ngāi Tahu chiefs. Also on board is a document called a deed – an agreement to buy and sell land. The largest amount of land to be sold as a block in Te Wai Pounamu. Will the chiefs sign? The year before, the Crown gets a big area of land by buying the Wairau district from three *North Island* chiefs; the Crown did not identify other right-holders to the land in the Wairau district. Māori want to keep mana over remaining land. The Crown tells Henry to 'reserve to the natives ample portions of land for their present and prospective wants'. The deed says Ngāi Tahu will get these reserves, plus schools and hospitals, plus mahinga kai areas will be set aside for them. Many pluses; Ngāi Tahu sign.


PHOTOCOPYING OF THIS PAGE IS RESTRICTED UNDER LAW.
ISBN: 9780170462419

How does that all work out? Godley arrives at Port Cooper (Lyttelton) in April 1850 with his wife and baby. He sees plans for three towns – Christchurch, Sumner and Lyttelton, and housing for settlers who will shortly arrive. He is said to be delighted. How delighted are Ngāi Tahu? Government agent Walter Mantell has mapped the land. The boundaries are unclear and promised reserves are reduced. Some cultivated land is not reserved for Ngāi Tahu as promised. Mahinga kai sites are limited to only areas cultivated as gardens or places of fixed structures such as eel weirs. Ngāi Tahu stare at poverty.

Things have not changed by 1877 when Te Maihāroa, a prophet said by some to perform miracles and who wants to regather mana Māori, leads over 100 people with horses, dogs and provisions up the Waitaki valley to set up a new settlement called Te Ao Mārama. They work the land, put up buildings, hold daily church services, set up a school, do not welcome Pākehā visitors. This makes some Pākehā runholders in the area suspicious and concerned. They complain, Your dogs worry our sheep, you worry us. Te Ao Mārama representatives go to Wellington to meet the Native Minister. We have a right to our land, they say. The Native Minister does not agree. He goes to Te Ao Mārama. Leave, go back to your reserves, he tells the people. They ignore him. Runholders keep complaining. The Native Minister issues an eviction order. He sends up 12 armed constables from Ōamaru who are reinforced with locals. You have 48 hours to leave, they tell Te Maihāroa. They arrest one of the settlement's leaders. Will violence erupt? No, Te Maihāroa takes the people back to the coast. But until he dies, he keeps petitioning the government to renegotiate the Kemp Deed and increase Māori reserves.

## Mahi Skills

1 **Local history:** An ancient proverb says a story is only half-told when one person tells it. Explain why it is important to hear more than one person's story of the selling and buying of the South Island.

2 **Exerting power:** Explain how the Kemp Deed is an example of one group exerting power over another and how that leads to resistance.

3 **Historical relationships:** Hōne Tikao is a chief who signs the Kemp Deed. Major Bunbury, who sails down to the South Island to collect signatures to the Treaty of Waitangi in 1840, describes him as very intelligent, well-dressed and an excellent speaker of English. Tikao's nephew provides knowledge to Pākehā historians. Tikao soon becomes unhappy with the allotment of reserves at Akaroa and argues about it. Show how his relationship with a formal document will be different to that of Henry Kemp's relationship with the same document.

4 **Thinking about government power:** Walter Mantell is said to become haunted by his broken promises to Ngāi Tahu. He appeals to officials in Britain and officials in New Zealand to fix things; later he agrees to become Native Minister on condition his promises to Ngāi Tahu are carried out and six months later when they are not, he resigns. Comment on what this suggests about government power.

5 **Interpreting past actions and decisions:** If you were asked to make an informed ethical judgement (using your own value system of what is right and wrong) about actions of Crown and Ngāi Tahu, list things you would need to consider.

# 30 Native Land Court

**Historians look at how laws affect people. When Government sets up the Native Land Court, many see it as an example of the Crown using its power to lessen Māori power. Some Māori and Pākehā say it is another act of war by settlers. Some say the wars are not getting enough land for settlers and so this is another way to get it. Some say it affects Māori more than any other colonial institution.**

The Native Land Court set up during the wars is for Māori to change customary land into individual land. On a request from Māori, it investigates which members own a block of land and those people get a certificate of title. Until 1873 the Court can name no more than ten owners of any block, big or small. Once ten people are named, other members cannot get certificates of title. At this time Māori and Pākehā still have different ideas about land ownership and use. Parliament is modelled on the ideas of the British Parliament. Therefore, when it passes Acts, it is thinking in terms of the British model of land ownership which means individual rather than communal holdings.

A Native Land Court hearing in the Far North.

When people want to state claims to land they have been living on, they have to travel in person to court and give evidence of belonging to the land and the land belonging to them. Judges who work in the Native Land Court are Pākehā. They have some Māori helpers. They meet at different places which can confuse; for example, some South Island cases are held in the North Island and many Waikato-Maniapoto cases are held in Auckland. Cases are often at isolated places, such as the Chatham Islands, or Taupō. Cases of the Rohe Pōtae case at Ōtorohanga last for three months in winter. Judge, helper and staff have to cross a flooded river in a waka, wade through mud and water, and sit for hours on a bench wrapped in overcoats and blankets.

Cases can go on for maybe several months. People have to find somewhere to stay and to eat – a hotel or camp at reserves or on riverbanks. This adds to costs of surveys, court fees, lawyers. In some cases the process takes all the money the land is worth. When Māori do not realise that their cases are being heard, the land can go to others.

*Airini Donnelly.*

Usually people behave well at hearings, but sometimes it gets heated. In the 1867 Mōtītī Island investigation a witness describes his chiefly opponents as liars. Rangatira say that more remarks like that will make them take up guns. The judge adjourns until people calm down.

Records show that some judges criticise the Government and do their best to protect Māori interests. The *New Zealand Herald* says, *men and women ... for the most part they have for years past lived in tents, or slept on the ground with the shelter merely of a break-wind. They have been made to do this by having to run from one part of the country to another after Land Courts. They have had to live on wretched watery food, such as potatoes, and the only relief from the utter misery of their surroundings is in getting drunk. What wonder is it that they should die of consumption ...* One MP says, *we could not devise a more ingenious method of destroying the whole of the Māori race than by these land courts.*

## Mahi Skills

1 **Local history:** Ngāti Kahungunu chief Rēnata Kawepō fights against Te Kooti at Te Pōrere during the wars. It is said a widow of a chief killed at Te Pōrere attacks Kawepō and takes out his eye. Kawepō will not let his people harm her. He marries her. Kawepō wins cases against land speculators in Hawke's Bay but has to sell much land to pay legal and living costs. One day he is sick and unable to plead a claim before the Native Land Court in Rangitīkei. His teenage great-niece Airini Donnelly persuades him to let her represent him and other claimants. She argues her case successfully. Use Kawepō and Airini as an example to explain how local areas have had people living there in the past with histories connected to the Native Land Court.

2 **Creating a visual:** Create a visual to show the different ideas of land-holding of Māori and Pākehā. Explain how Government is aiming to change one idea.

3 **Star diagram:** Make a star diagram about the Native Land Court.

4 **Gathering information:** Today the Māori Land Court (Te Kooti Whenua Māori) is about recognising the importance of Māori land as a taonga tuku iho for iwi to tell their histories. Gather some information about it to show how it differs from the original.

5 **Understanding empathy:** Empathy is being aware of what another is experiencing. Decide if there is evidence here of any Pākehā empathy and give reasons for your decision.

# 31 Pai Mārire

**Historians look at how people respond as individuals or groups to challenges in their communities. One way some Māori respond to the wars is by following new prophets and religions which aim to make sense of what is happening. One new religion is Pai Mārire – goodness and peace. Its church is called Hauhau – the breath of God. People use both Pai Mārire and Hauhau for this religion.**

*Te Ua Haumēne.*

The founder of Pai Mārire is Te Ua Haumēne of Taranaki and Te Āti Awa. In the 1820s Waikato capture him and take him to Kawhia to be a slave. Now he is back in Taranaki. He is against the sale of Māori land. He is for Kīngitanga. He believes Māori have the right to defend their rohe. He fights Crown forces in Taranaki. He thinks missionaries may be a cause of Māori losing land. He believes it is his job to lead Māori to cast off the Pākehā yoke. He holds ceremonies involving chants and circling a niu, a tall pole with three flags – the Riki flag for war, the Ruru flag for peace and a flag for the priest.

On 6 April 1864 Hauhau ambush soldiers resting near Ōakura during a mission to destroy Māori crops. They take the head of one of the seven dead soldiers around the North Island to encourage people to join Pai Mārire.

Near New Plymouth, soldiers build a redoubt on the ancient pā site of Te Mōrere (Sentry Hill) on Te Āti Awa land. Two mortars and 75 to 100 soldiers defend it. Several hundred Pai Mārire attack on 30 April 1864. One is a 12-year-old boy. He carries a gun for the first time. Later he describes what happens. Early in the morning at Manutahi pā the taua does its ceremonies around the niu pole. Leaders carry tokotoko, special staffs; their followers have muskets, shotguns, tomahawks, stone patu, taiaha, mānuka spears. The taua marches through forest and into fern and tutu bush in front of the redoubt. The plan is a rear attack but at 8 am the chiefs instead march them up the hill. They chant Pai Mārire words. Is it true what some say, that they think this will stop bullets? Hidden soldiers open fire. They kill about 35 and wound others. The boy bathes his shoulder and hip wounds in a stream and escapes into the bush.

Some upriver Whanganui Māori get involved in Pai Mārire. On 14 May 1864 they set out to attack Whanganui town. Downriver Māori intercept them. The two groups agree to fight it out on Moutoa Island in the middle of the river. Maybe not strictly a battle between Kīngitanga supporters and Crown supporters, but more a battle over whether one group can use the river to attack Pākehā?


PHOTOCOPYING OF THIS PAGE IS RESTRICTED UNDER LAW.
ISBN: 9780170462419

*Hauhau ceremony. The artist is soldier with guide on right whom Hauhau captured but let go.*

Not so much about protecting Pākehā as protecting the mana of the river? In the fighting, the downriver group loses fewer warriors. A short battle but it is said to cast a long shadow on the river. The two groups will join together in 1869 on the river in a fleet of waka to chase guerrilla leader Te Kooti who evades them.

Even though beaten in battle, Pai Mārire keeps spreading. In early October 1866, Ngāti Hineuru chief Te Rangihiroa and Pai Mārire prophet Panapa lead a taua towards Napier and into Ōmarunui kāinga at Tūtaekurī River. Most kāinga people have gone to a nearby pā. Just after midnight on 12 October, militia march out of Napier. A party of Ngāti Kahungunu join them. By daybreak they have nearly surrounded Ōmarunui. They invite the people to surrender. Nothing happens. They open fire. Most defenders who try to escape are captured, wounded or killed. The remaining raise a white flag. Ceasefire. Official statistics are two soldiers killed and nine wounded, two Ngāti Kahungunu killed and four wounded. It is thought 23 Ngāti Hineuru dead are buried in the pā, and about another 30 are wounded. Panapa is dead. Any Ngāti Hineuru survivors who can walk are marched to Napier. The wounded get taken to hospital. Others get exiled to the Chatham Islands.

## Mahi Skills

1 **Local history:** Some Pākehā accounts describe putting children to bed in their clothes and training them to get up silently in the middle of the night. Explain why they might have done this and find out if there was a Hauhau presence in your local area.

2 **Matching:** Rewrite the following into matching pairs. *Breath of God, founder, goodness and peace, Hauhau, Moutoa, Ōmarunui, Pai Mārire, Riki, Ruru, Sentry Hill, staff, Te Morere, Te Ua Haumēne, tokotoko, Tūtaekurī River, Whanganui.*

3 **Developing theories:** Put forward some theories that might explain the following. *Pai Mārire gets converts even though their chants do not stop enemy bullets. A severed head is used as a recruitment aid.*

4 **Responses:** Describe some challenges to which Pai Mārire may have been a response.

5 **Problem-solving:** You download an image of Māori with a flag and memorial presented to them by townspeople but then forget where the image is taken. Work out the location.

ISBN: 9780170462419 PHOTOCOPYING OF THIS PAGE IS RESTRICTED UNDER LAW. 

# 32 East Coast

**Historians look at choices people make such as whether or not to join a group, and how those choices impact on them. East Coast Māori are generally fine with Pākehā traders bringing goods but not so much with the idea of Pākehā settlements in their area. When Governor Browne visits Poverty Bay in 1860, locals tell him Queen Victoria is not their ruler. This does not mean they rush to support Māori forces elsewhere. War, however, comes for them.**

Te Whakatōhea iwi has coastal settlements around Ōpōtiki and has built a church and school for missionary Carl Völkner in Ōpōtiki. In early 1865 the iwi pledges support to Kīngitanga. They lose warriors in skirmishes around the coast, suffer food shortages, and lose people to typhoid and measles. Carl Völkner has been visiting Auckland. Māori warn him not to come back because some people think he is a Government spy. He comes back to Ōpōtiki.

Revd C.S. Volkener
Murdered by Hauhaus Opotiki
Mar. 2 1865

Pai Mārire agents who arrive in February include Kereopa Te Rau who fought in Kīngitanga forces in Waikato. It is believed his wife and two daughters were killed at Rangiaowhia and his sister was killed at Hairini next day. Agents convert many Te Whakatōhea. On 2 March 1865 Māori take Carl Völkner to a tree near the church, hang him and cut off his head. Kereopa swallows the eyes. One eye is Parliament, he says. The other is the British Queen and law. The Reverend Grace from Taupō has fled to Ōpōtiki after Pai Mārire ransack his house. Hauhau try to swap him for a Tauranga chief who is in prison. The reverend escapes to a British gunship which is standing offshore. In a letter to the Crown, Māori say they kill Völkner because missionaries are trying to get Māori land and the head of the Anglican Church is said to be holding services for the British Army, and the Governor killed women at Rangiriri and Rangiaowhia.

Hemi Te Mautaranui (James Fulloon), son of John Fulloon and the daughter of a Ngāti Awa and Tūhoe leader, convinces the Governor to let him recruit a company of Ngāti Awa to catch the killers of Völkner. He arrives at Whakatāne on a ship. On 22 July, a group including Ngāti Awa, go aboard and kill Fulloon and two crew. In August, a Crown force goes into the rohe of Ngāti Awa to arrest people for the murders. They destroy kāinga and waka, take cattle and horses, and skirmish with Ngāti Awa.

In September the Crown says that the war which began in Taranaki is at an end. It pardons those who fought against the Crown but not those who killed Fulloon. If the killers are not given up, the Crown will take some lands of those tribes who hide them. Crown forces lay siege to pā at Matatā, Whakatāne and Te Teko. On 17 May 1866 in Auckland, two Māori are hanged for the murder of Fulloon and crew and three for the murder of Völkner. Kereopa goes into Te Urewera.


PHOTOCOPYING OF THIS PAGE IS RESTRICTED UNDER LAW.
ISBN: 9780170462419

Hanging of Carl Völkner.

Tūranga (Gisborne) iwi also see the need to stay home and look after their own land when war breaks out in Taranaki. They do not join Kīngitanga as they have their own ariki. When Pai Mārire arrives in March 1865 many Tūranga Māori adopt it. Although Pai Mārire say they want peace, many settlers leave. Some Ngāti Porou are for Pai Mārire, some are divided, some are against, and in June, some are helped by Crown troops to attack their Pai Mārire members.

In September Crown troops arrive at Tūranga. Waerenga-a-Hika pā is pro-Pai Mārire and has several hundred people sheltering from the wars. Government agent Donald McLean wants it gone. He writes, I am not bloodthirsty but I hope our enemies will now begin to feel our power and soon see the necessity of yielding to British prowess and skill. He gets volunteers from Ngāti Porou and takes them down by steamer to join his troops. On 9 November he tells Waerenga-a-Hika pā, Get rid of Pai Mārire agents, hand over people who fought against Government, hand over arms, take the oath of allegiance, compensate settlers for damage to property. If you don't, you will be attacked and lose your land. Pai Mārire reply in a letter that they are willing to accept terms if Donald McLean will come to see them. He will not. The deadline passes. On 16 November the Crown force attacks Waerenga-a-Hika. Six days of shooting and fighting and artillery and then the people of Waerenga-a-Hika put down their arms. Historians think they are tired, have not wanted to fight, do not want to see any more killed, believe the promise that most will be allowed to stay in the area. Estimated deaths are 11 Crown fighters and at least 71 from the pā, and about 100 wounded. Hundreds are taken prisoner and exiled without trial to Wharekauri. They will soon be joined by Te Kooti, who fights with Crown forces at Waerenga-a-Hika but will become a dreaded enemy to Government. Escapees from Waerenga-a-Hika, along with Pai Mārire refugees, go south into Te Urewera. Government can now confiscate land and open up the East Coast to Pākehā settlement.

## Mahi Skills

1 **Local history:** Hauhau arriving in the East Cape area leads to intertribal conflict. Explain how and why it shows how complex local history can be.

2 **Listening to music:** In 2016 the New Zealand Youth Choir perform overseas at the International Festival of Academic Choirs. They win gold in all their categories and win the overall grand prize. One song they perform is *Waerenga-a-Hika* composed by Tuirina Wehi from the East Coast. It leaves audience and judges in tears. Listen to the song.

3 **Values interpretation:** Donald McLean, a Scotsman, is said to have a good understanding of Māori culture and insists settlers, some of whom he calls scum of the earth, honour agreements with Māori. Yet he comes to think the best chance for Māori is assimilation. Describe how he and his values might be called a product of the times.

4 **Understanding macrons:** A macron is a straight bar symbol over a vowel (a, e, i, o, u) to show you need to pronounce it as a long vowel. It is used in other languages besides Māori. Make a list of words from this chapter with macrons.

5 **Writing an abstract:** Imagine you have written an article about the killing of Völkner at Waerenga-a-Hika pā and want to preface it with an abstract – a summary of your article. Write an abstract of about half a page.

# 33 The Chute March

**Historians sometimes use revisionism. This means they revise their attitude to a previously accepted idea about something or someone. They know that history is about the present and past talking to each other. They know there is not one rigid and right idea about people and events of the past. New evidence and new interpretations can make them have a rethink. An example is Major Chute. Generally most, but not all, colonists and newspapers hail him as a hero during the New Zealand Wars. Generally today most, but not all, people think many of his actions are not those of a hero.**

General Cameron resigns in August 1865 and leaves New Zealand. He has tried to convince the Colonial Office in London to pull out British troops from New Zealand. The British army does most of the fighting, he says, and has the most killed and wounded in order for settlers to take Māori land. Many of his soldiers also admire Māori courage and kindness to wounded soldiers.

GENERAL CHUTE.

Major-General Trevor Chute arrives to replace Cameron as commander of the British forces. On his first visit to New Zealand his regiment helped build the military road from Auckland to the Waikato. Now he comes to Taranaki to remove Māori from the bush alongside a planned Taranaki–Whanganui road.

There is supposed to be peace in Taranaki but Māori are reacting to the land confiscations by ambushing and killing soldiers and settlers. Chute is here to stop Taranaki resisting British sovereignty.

On 30 December 1865 he sets out from Whanganui for six weeks with 620 soldiers which include about 270 Māori, detachments of Forest Rangers and artillery, and Transport Corps driving two-horse drays.

His aim is to attack pā and destroy kāinga and their livestock in South Taranaki and drive Māori out.

This policy of sudden attacks on soft targets is called bush-scouring. It involves searching for Māori in the bush and attacking their kāinga and cultivations so they will fight. Some historians say it is also scorched earth policy – destroying anything that might be useful to an enemy.

*The Chute march starts at Ketemarae.*

On 17 January 1866 Chute launches another campaign. He gathers a force of about 500 including Forest Rangers and a Native Contingent, and 90 horses.

This time he is going to march his troops to New Plymouth through the bush on the eastern side of Mt Taranaki.

He has been in New Zealand for only a few months so it sounds better in a plan than in real life.

Māori say they can do the ancient 54-mile war-track he chooses in two days.

Chute takes nine days. Undergrowth is thick. Rain pours down. He has taken packhorses and the terrain has many rivers and many gullies. His troops have to make bridges. He gets lost. He takes rations for three days. His men are starving and have to eat a dog and two of their horses.

On 1 February, after they recover, the troops march off by the coastal route to Whanganui to finish the circumnavigation of Mt Taranaki.

One politician says there are 'avoidable cruelties'. A letter comes from the London Colonial Office, which has read Governor Grey's reports expressing satisfaction with the Chute campaign. It says, I doubt whether the natives have ever attempted to devastate our settlements as we are devastating theirs. There is more destruction than fighting.

However, Chute gets big congratulations for such a triumph. New Plymouth settlers say he has conquered the interior. At a Wellington banquet the Governor praises Chute's 'restoration of peace and tranquillity in a previously dangerous district'.

The Auckland *Southern Cross* newpaper says Chute has shown uncommon energy, hardihood and determination and shown Māori that the bush does not stop troops, that they can struggle through its swamps and gullies and tangled supplejack. Chute, it says, has destroyed the security Māori have in the bush and also the prestige of the bush. He has shown Māori that there is nowhere they can go where British power cannot track them out. In 1866 military settlers begin taking possession of land confiscated from Taranaki Māori.

Surveyors work on the land, a military camp is set up at Pātea, Māori raid parties and convoys, Crown forces raid local villages and destroy crops.

Fighting ends in November. There is an uneasy peace.

Until June 1868 and a man called Tītokowaru sets Taranaki alight again.

## Mahi Skills

1 **Local history:** Chute's reports include opinions. For example, he labels Te Pūtahi pā Māori as 'two hundred rebels of the worst character'. Chute will soon leave New Zealand for good. Create five questions about the effect Chute had, that you could ask local iwi if they gave you permission.

2 **Imagining:** Imagine you are one of Chute's party on his march around Mt Taranaki and prepare a diary entry. You might do some research (paperspast.natlib.govt.nz) and read newspaper reports of the time such as the *Nelson Examiner* saying, *There were no prisoners made in these late engagements as General Chute ... doesn't care to encumber himself with such costly luxuries.*

3 **Recognising how beliefs affect actions:** Use the picture of Chute in his British Army uniform to help explain why he held his beliefs at that time and how they could have helped cause him to act as he did.

4 **Understanding how images can be idealised:** Idealising means showing an event as perfect or at least as better than it was. Make a comment about why historians suggest the watercolour by Gustavus von Tempsky is idealised. Then decide which figure in the painting is the artist.

5 **Assessing:** Read the following and assess the chances that the woman in the painting is Lucy Takiora Lord.

*Lucy is from Kororāreka and has a Māori mother and Pākehā father. Just before the Northern War begins, her mother, a former slave, mentions Hōne Heke in relation to a pig's head. Heke and his followers loot the Lords' home, store and butcher's shop and capture Lucy's mother. Lucy marries Te Mahuki from Whanganui and they act as guides and interpreters for Crown military forces. They often work with Gustavus von Tempsky and feature in his paintings.*


PHOTOCOPYING OF THIS PAGE IS RESTRICTED UNDER LAW.
ISBN: 9780170462419

# Tītokowaru 34

**Historians try to explain mysteries. Tītokowaru from Ngāti Ruahine is born in Taranaki. He has mana; he is mentioned as a Māori King candidate. He is a genius military engineer and leader; he damages Crown forces and morale so much that it is said Government thinks of giving back confiscated land and making peace with Te Kooti, another big enemy, so it can concentrate on fighting Tītokowaru. For many historians, Tītokowaru is a man of mystery.**

Was Tītokowaru trained as a tohunga when younger? Why, even though a war expert, does he usually direct operations rather than use weapons? Why does he support setting up a Māori King and later give up supporting Kīngitanga? Why does he want peace and also fight with Pai Mārire? Why does he defend Māori land yet say, As for the lands, let them go, I wish to live in peace? Is it a bullet or shell splinter that blinds his eye? Why does he have a reputation for having no mercy yet is also known for being friendly and hospitable, and sparing some enemy Pākehā? Does he really say the Governor is worth way less than the Governor's bounty on his, Tītokowaru's, head?

*Tītokowaru.*

Tītokowaru declares 1867 a year of peace. After being entertained at the Crown base of Camp Waihi on 10 June, he leads followers on a peace march that ends at Pipiriki on Whanganui River. Near Ōkaiawa he builds Te Ngutu-o-te-manu – the beak of the bird. There are over 50 houses, a big marae, meeting house and a peace centre. He gives up support for Kīngitanga and oversees non-violent resistance to confiscation of land. In March 1868 he authorises a muru against a Pākehā over land confiscation at Ketemarae (Normanby). A Crown force raids Te Ngutu-o-te-manu to get back plunder, and imprison some of Tītokowaru's men. One escapes. Tītokowaru refuses to hand him over. He goes to war instead. Most fighting is in the coastal area between Whanganui and Mt Taranaki. The mostly confiscated land contains scrub, thick bush and some open country.

ISBN: 9780170462419
PHOTOCOPYING OF THIS PAGE IS RESTRICTED UNDER LAW.

Government sends Armed Constables and Te Keepa's Whanganui Māori to Taranaki. Tītokowaru is terrifying the settlers. Is it just the raids and ambushes, the stealing and the burning of buildings that force settlers to leave farms? Does his great white horse — Niu Tīrene — help with the idea he is a superhero who can control artillery shells and wind? Is it the letter he writes advising Pākehā to keep off roads as he has begun to eat the flesh of white people? Is it because nobody has pictures of him so he is said to go around Whanganui ready to pounce on unsuspecting settlers? Is it because he revives the whāngai hau ritual where the heart of a slain enemy is cut out and offered to Tūmatauenga, god of war?

On 12 July 1868 about 60 warriors, with deserter soldier Charles Kane, leave Te Ngutu-o-te-manu, bypass Waihi soldiers and before dawn attack the Turuturu-mōkai redoubt. They kill ten soldiers and cut out the heart of one. Major McDonnell, who can speak te reo Māori, is said to have kissed the blade of his sword and said, I shall have revenge for this. On 21 August Armed Constabulary attack Te Ngutu-o-te-manu. It stands. They attack again on 7 September. Warriors hide in the forest. They open fire. They kill 24 including Major Gustavus von Tempsky. On 7 November a Crown force including Māori from Whanganui under Te Rangihiwinui Keepa attack Tītokowaru at Moturoa. The Crown force loses 19 men, Tītokowaru loses one.

Tītokowaru begins work on Taurangaika pā. He has about 400 fighters. Nearly 2000 soldiers protect Whanganui. In late January 1869 the Armed Constabulary camp close to the pā. They begin digging trenches and an Armstrong gun opens fire. At sunrise of 3 February troops find the Taurangaika people have left during the night. Why does Tītokowaru's army suddenly break up? Do they run out of food or ammo? Is it a strategic withdrawal or fear of the coming attack? Tītokowaru loses mana by having an affair with a married woman? Is Tītokowaru worried the west coast will get flooded with soldiers if he keeps winning battles?

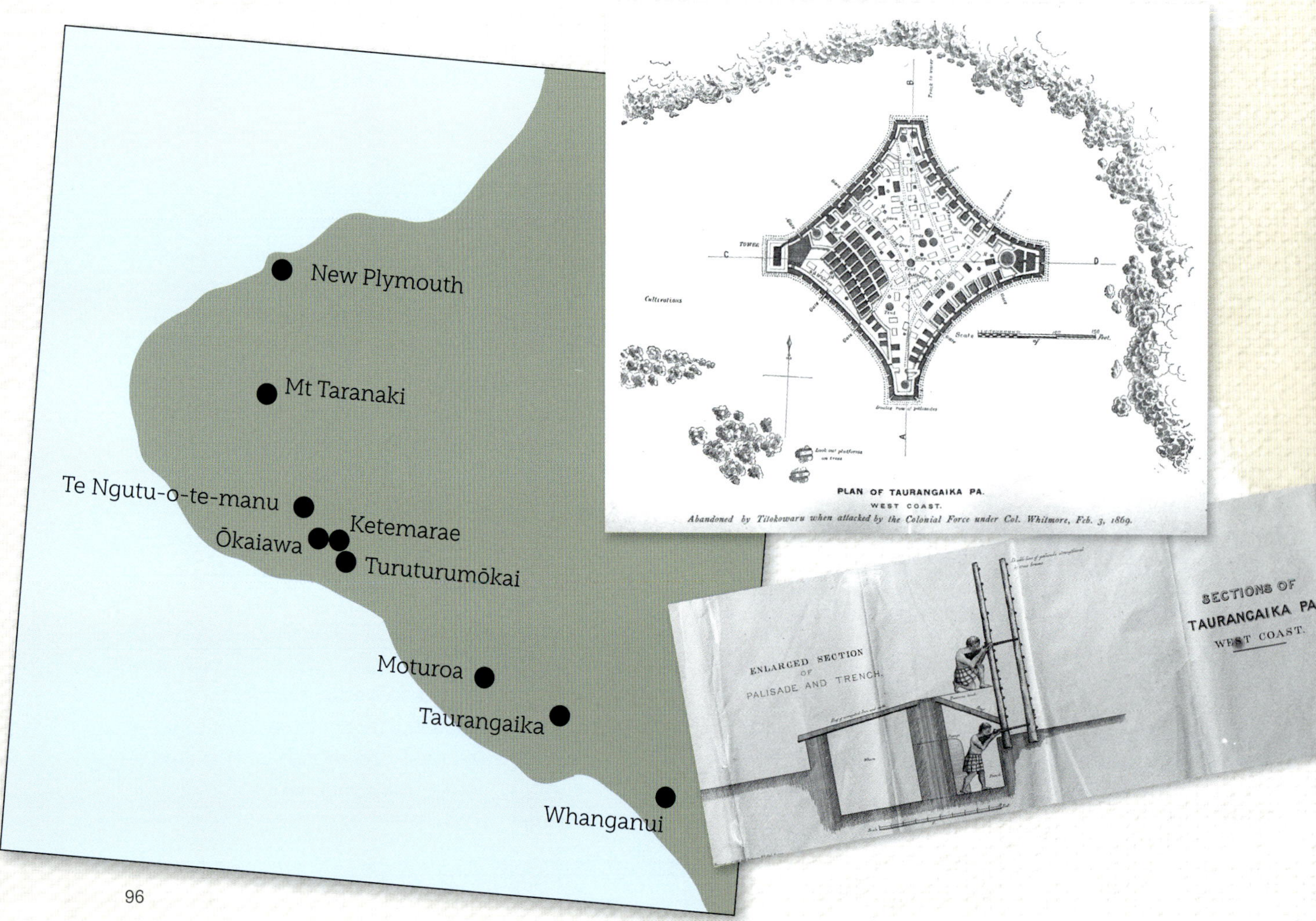

For weeks Crown forces search for Tītokowaru. When they catch up with him he evades capture, and then does it again. He disappears into the upper Waitara Valley in North Taranaki. But that is not the end of him. He will be seen again at Parihaka.

*Attack on Te Ngutu-o-te-manu.*

## Mahi Skills

1 **Local history:** Work out which iwi and hapū are the ones who hold knowledge of Tītokowaru. Give reasons for your decision.

2 **Activating prior knowledge:** Historians suggest Tītokowaru may see three-year-old John Guard who lives with Ngāti Ruanui as a captive for a while. Check your memory of the Guard story and that of Tītokowaru honouring von Tempsky at Te Ngutu-o-te-manu. Note how well you do.

3 **Listing:** Make a list of things about Tītokowaru's actions and beliefs that may puzzle Pākehā during the wars.

4 **Understanding a design:** Explain why Taurangaika, which Tītokowaru uses as a base to launch raids on farms and military posts, is often called a masterpiece.

5 **Critical thinking:** This is the letter from Tītokowaru to Colonel Whitmore, delivered by two Māori who get called rebels and put in jail. Explain in your own words the message Tītokowaru is delivering.

> *To whom does England belong? To whom does this place belong on which you are standing? … You were made a Pākehā and England was made for you. I was made a Māori and New Zealand was made for me. You did not recollect that a great division was made between us, the great sea. You ceased to remember this fact and crossed over from that place to this. I did not jump over from this place to that. My word to you. Move out of my place to your own places in the midst of the sea. Clear out of the town and all other places … Tītokowaru.*

# 35 Te Kooti

Historians understand that for some people Te Kooti is a violent rebel and for others a spiritual leader. Divided loyalties among Māori during the wars also – Māori as well as Crown forces chase him through the central North Island as he wages guerrilla warfare, and when he escapes into Te Urewera, Tūhoe decide to support him at a formal commitment in their Waimana Valley.

When most of his Ngāti Maru hapū convert to Pai Mārire, Te Kooti does not and he founds a Ringatū faith whose influence lives on in places including the eastern Bay of Plenty and East Coast.

When he dodges his chasers and gets in to the King Country, the Government cannot reach him and he dedicates the rest of his life to peace, law, religion – and also to the message of getting Māori land back.

Te Kooti Arikirangi Te Turuki from Poverty Bay Rongowhakaata iwi has a long campaign against settlers and the Crown and despite many hunters is never caught. There are many stories about Te Kooti – that his father rejects him as a youth and buries him alive in a kūmara pit or well, that he gets a reputation as a tearaway, that he hangs out with and leads young men who take Pākehā possessions as utu for grievances, that he has many wives, that he has skills in horsemanship and handling boats and trading, that he gets powerful enemies. He is known as a fierce fighter, a guerrilla warfare specialist, leading small groups against a bigger and less mobile enemy to sabotage, ambush, raid. His patrols sweep in hit-and-runs, capture supplies, horses, arms, ammunition.

There are stories of miraculous escapes from bullets and capture, of his white horse with spiritual powers to make sure its rider is never caught. Even though he is not Pai Mārire, Government says he sells gunpowder to Hauhau and suspect he is a spy. They ship him off to Wharekauri (Chatham Islands) with other 'trouble-makers'.

*In the far distance is Ngātapa pā, mountain-top fortress.*

At Wharekauri he becomes a spiritual leader, makes prophecies such as the return of Māori land, has bouts of fever and visions, holds religious services where he rubs phosphorus from matches so it seems flames come from his hands. On 4 July 1868 he leads an escape where prisoners seize a supply ship. Winds are bad during the voyage back to New Zealand. A sacrifice is needed. People put taonga in a blanket and throw it over the side. It does not work. But it is said a good breeze comes when they throw Te Kooti's uncle, believed to be a Government spy, overboard. On 10 July 1868 they land at Whareongaonga.


PHOTOCOPYING OF THIS PAGE IS RESTRICTED UNDER LAW.
ISBN: 9780170462419

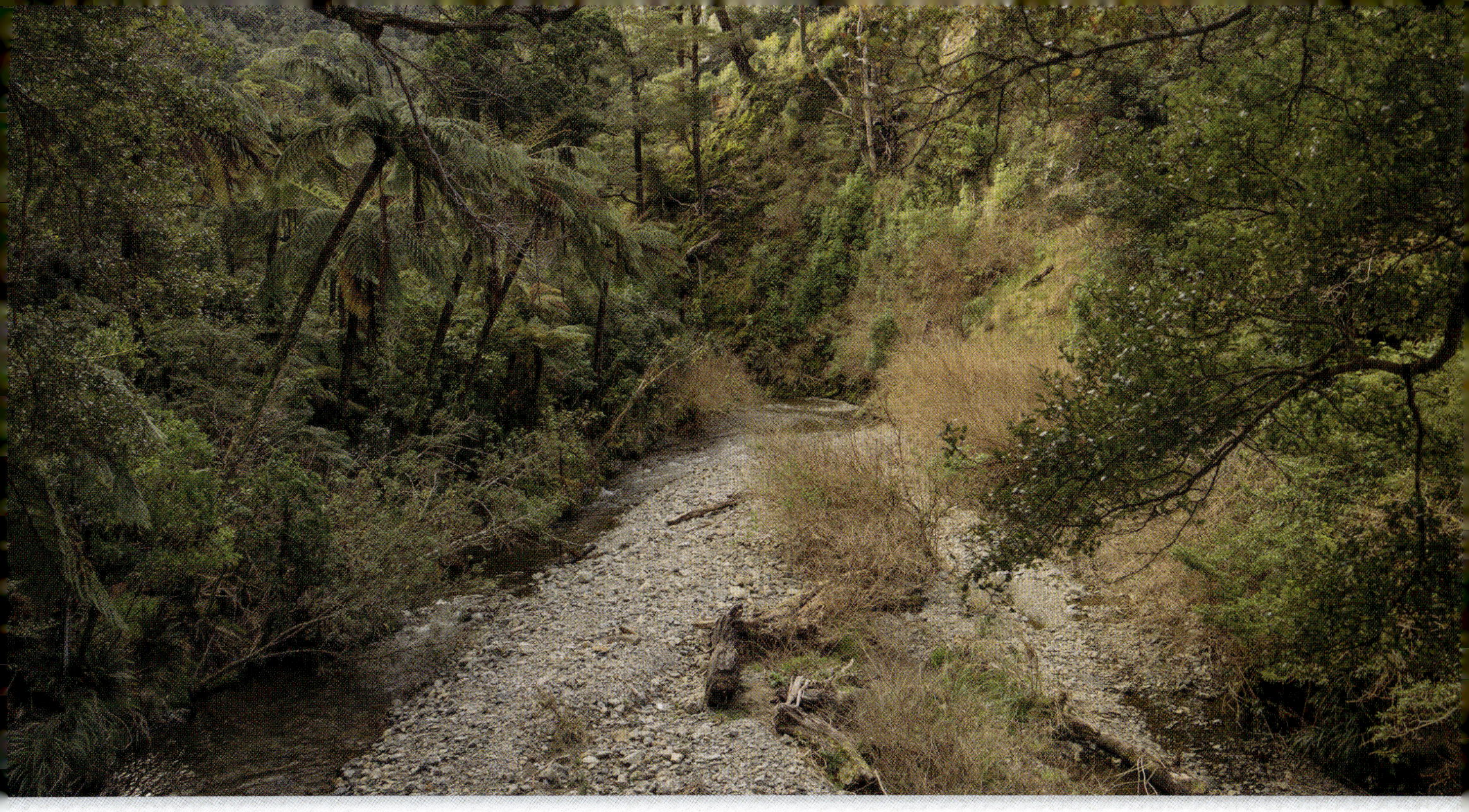

After Te Arawa Flying Column chase Te Kooti from Ōhinemutu at Lake Rotorua in an eight-mile running battle, Te Kooti escapes into Te Urewera and Government offers a reward for his capture.

Reginald Biggs, Resident Magistrate at Poverty Bay and the army officer who exiled Te Kooti, hears Te Kooti is back. He sends three Māori to tell him to give up his arms and surrender. Te Kooti says he and the whakarau (exiles) want only to be left alone and will fight only if chased and attacked. Biggs gathers volunteers and Māori allies to go and capture Te Kooti. On 9 November at about midnight Te Kooti and his followers, many on horseback, attack Matawhero. They torch homes, kill an estimated 50 to 60 Pākehā, including the Biggs family. Te Kooti now has unfinished business with Rongowhakaata chief Paratene Tūrangi at Oweta pā. Paratene is said to have mocked Te Kooti when he was exiled or to have urged authorities to exile Te Kooti. Paratene has returned his arms to Government. He visits Te Kooti at Patutahi to ask him not to kill any more. Te Kooti tries to pressure Rongowhakaata into joining him. On 12 November Te Kooti and his followers go to Oweta pā. They kill Paratene Tūrangi and several others.

Te Kooti goes to the ancient hill-top pā of Ngātapa which has cliffs on three sides, dense bush on the other, and no easy water supply. He has many followers but fewer warriors. On 5 December Armed Constabulary and Māori allies attack. Te Kooti sends the attackers off. Another attack on 1 January 1869 and then a siege. One night Te Kooti and his fighters use bush vines to escape down cliffs. When attackers enter the pā on 6 January they find only women and children. For two days they chase and capture people in bush and gorges below the pā and bring the prisoners back to their camp at Ngātapa. No Te Kooti. Many witnesses say that large numbers of prisoners are led to the edge of the cliff, stripped, shot, and thrown over the cliff. The exact number is still debated. The Crown says maybe eight and points blame at Māori allies. Later the Waitangi Tribunal will say between 86 and 128. Te Kooti and his remaining followers escape into Te Urewera. Units of Māori and Armed Constabulary chase them.

Some claim Pacific's triple star in the national anthem is Te Kooti's flag because the Irishman who writes it supports Te Kooti's stand against the Crown.

In March and April 1869 Te Kooti raids Whakatāne and Mōhaka. It is said he kills 60, mostly Māori, at Mōhaka. In June 1869 he and his followers leave Te Urewera and in July arrive at Te Kuiti where the Māori King is. He knows he can go there only in peace but he tells them to hold the land and keep fighting. The Māori King does not meet him. At Te Pōrere near Tongariro, Te Kooti builds a British-style redoubt. On 4 October 1869 an Armed Constabulary force from Whanganui, joined by Māori, fight Te Kooti there. They kill 37 of his men and capture about 30. Te Kooti escapes although he loses two fingers in the fighting.

*Some of the Armed Constabulary here at Tūranga in 1868 may have fought at Ngātapa.*

On 16 January 1870 Te Kooti is at the Waikato village of Tapapa. He meets settler Josiah Firth. If left alone I won't fight again, he is said to tell Firth. Firth pleads his case with Government. The Premier's message to Te Kooti is, If you surrender you will be given safe passage to Auckland – as a prisoner. He says Te Kooti is 'a midnight murderer of defenceless women and helpless children ... a man of atrocious cruelty and outrage'. The Native Minister decides that the chase to get Te Kooti will be left to Māori. A big reward is offered for his capture. Expeditions into Te Urewera in January 1871 fail to get Te Kooti. In May 1872 Te Kooti goes again to the King Country. This time he gets to live at Te Kuiti. On 12 February 1883 he meets the Native Minister and they exchange pledges of peace. He is pardoned but not allowed to return to Poverty Bay.

## Mahi Skills

1. **Local history:** List places where Te Kooti may appear in local histories.
2. **Finding details:** Accounts of Te Kooti's escape from the Chathams suggest military precision. Find out details.
3. **Persevering:** Use the following to comment on why there is always something else to find out about events and people.

> *Te Kooti claims he shot two Hauhau at Waerenga-a-Hika but rangatira Paora Parau accuses him of giving gunpowder to Hauhau. Arrested as a spy on 21 November, he has to be released when there is no proof. In March 1866 authorities re-arrest him on a charge of warning a local Pai Mārire chief that military action is coming. No trial and Te Kooti is shipped off.*

4. **Understanding changing relationships:** Arawa are one of the kūpapa forces who chase Te Kooti; in the late 1880s they build a prayer house for him when he visits the Rotorua district. Explain the changing relationship.
5. **Advertising:** Find and comment on the poster advertising the 1927 film *The Te Kooti Trail.*


PHOTOCOPYING OF THIS PAGE IS RESTRICTED UNDER LAW.
ISBN: 9780170462419

# Te Urewera 36

**Historians understand people move between places. They know Māori are considered to be mobile. They know that movements between places have results for both places and people. It is largely people moving into Te Urewera that involve Tūhoe in the wars.**

Te Urewera (burnt penis) in the 19th century is majestic, mysterious, inland, isolated. Forests, hills, mountains, rivers, lakes, foot tracks, no roads. Much of it is in Hawke's Bay, some in eastern Bay of Plenty. People live mostly in valleys and clearings with little farming land. It can get cold. Kūmara grows in only some places. Ngāi Tūhoe iwi there connect with the land. It is said their ancestors are Te Maunga (mountain) and Hine-pukohu-rangi (Mist Maiden). They are sometimes called Ngā Tamariki o te Kohu – Children of the Mist. Maungapōhatu is their sacred mountain, Lake Waikaremoana is their ancestral bathing waters. They did not sign the Treaty of Waitangi; the iwi say it was not given the chance. They say they never gave up sovereignty.

Until the 1860s the Crown has no official presence there. Few Pākehā visit. There are no Pākehā settlements, no Crown lands, no Crown building. Rewi Maniapoto of Ngāti Maniapoto visits looking for allies for the Waikato war. A Tūhoe party of men, women and children go to Waikato. They fight at Ōrākau. Their 60 per cent casualties includes their rangatira Piripi Te Heuheu.

The Völkner killing brings Kereopa into Te Urewera looking for safety. The Crown is after him. It accuses Tūhoe of being in rebellion against the Crown. Not true, say Tūhoe. Later the Waitangi Tribunal will say Tūhoe were not involved in the killings of Völkner or Fulloon. For a while some Tūhoe see mana in Kereopa as an apostle of Pai Mārire and then some Tūhoe are attracted to Te Kooti's Ringatū faith. Yet they do not tell the Crown where Kereopa is. But he threatens their survival. They withdraw protection. In September 1871 they take him to Ruatāhuna, and hand him over to Pākehā Captain Porter and Ngāti Porou leader Major Rāpata Wahawaha who has been fighting against Pai Mārire.

After Waerenga-a-Hika some Pai Mārire come to Lake Waikaremoana. Crown forces chase them. In January 1866 the Crown sends a messenger to Waikaremoana rangatira. If you want to spare your lives, says the message, give up Hauhauism, give up arms and swear the oath of allegiance. They take the messenger prisoner, and later kill and decapitate him. Another Crown expedition comes in. It is mostly kūpapa. They attack Tūhoe at Te Kopani on the southern shore of Lake Waikaremoana and kill maybe 40–50. They destroy kāinga, take horses and cattle, wreck crops. At Onepoto redoubt at Lake Waikaremoana, Major Rāpata Wahawaha is said to have shot four prisoners.

Some Tūhoe land is included in the Bay of Plenty confiscated land. Tūhoe do not send Te Kooti away when he arrives after Ngātapa. The Crown force of Armed Constabulary and kūpapa old enemies of Tūhoe, who come after Te Kooti, outnumber the whole population of Te Urewera. The force carries out raids on Tūhoe. The head of the Armed Constabulary writes in an official report that when his men are off-duty they roam about the country foraging, destroying crops, burning kāinga, and seeking the enemy's scouts. He is sorry that all the rebels could not be killed. He hands over Tūhoe women and children prisoners to Te Arawa. At Lake Waikaremoana, an officer says he is pleased his men have destroyed potatoes that would have fed 1000 men for 15 months. Women, children and elderly are kept at Te Putere. They have no seeds or tools to grow food, no boats for fishing. Crown forces kill some Tūhoe collecting kai near Te Whata-a-pona pā.

In 1871 Tūhoe reach an agreement with the Crown. They will lay down their arms and help capture Te Kooti if the Crown forces stop the scorched earth policy. Te Kooti escapes unharmed to the King Country.

There is still unrest in Te Urewera. Some Pākehā think there is gold there. It should be opened for prospectors and settlers, they say. Some Tūhoe chiefs apply for a survey of a block of land. It is thought the reason is to stop it being surveyed on behalf of traditional enemies. Other Tūhoe oppose the survey. Conflict follows, including Tūhoe taking away surveying instruments, sending surveyors away, taking down trig stations, taking axes from Māori contracted to cut survey lines through bush, armed police and troops arriving, Tūhoe chiefs and some women being arrested, and MPs acting as mediators. Although the situation calms, the relationship between Tūhoe and Crown is strained.

By the time World War 1 arrives in 1914 the relationship between Government and Te Urewera is further strained. At the centre is a Tūhoe prophet, said to be the son of a Ngāti Kahungunu man killed fighting for Te Kooti. His name is Rua Kēnana and he claims he is the One who Te Kooti predicted would come after him to finish Te Kooti's work by getting the land back. Rua says he must do certain tasks. For example, one is to go into the sacred meeting house of Rongopai at Poverty Bay built to receive Te Kooti although Government arrests him to stop him going to its opening; the story is that Rua gets into the locked house with help from Te Kooti's white horse.

*Rua Kēnana.*

Rua builds a community at the foot of Maungapōhatu to be separate from Government and its organisation. His spiritual faith and followers are Iharaira (Israelites). The circular meeting house is 'parliament'. There is an agreement that Tūhoe and other Urewera iwi can keep governing themselves if they recognise the authority of the Crown. Māori want the agreement to include a ban on land sales but the Crown reserves the right of buying land to itself. When Rua needs money to develop Maungapōhatu, he is willing to sell a limited area to Government to get the money.


PHOTOCOPYING OF THIS PAGE IS RESTRICTED UNDER LAW.
ISBN: 9780170462419

It is tough living at Maungapōhatu with poor winters, poor diet, poor housing. And Government keeps watching Rua. It passes a law aimed largely at Rua to replace traditional tohunga healers with Western medicine. In 1908 Rua goes to meet Prime Minister Joseph Ward on the beach at Whakatāne. He asks for a Māori government. There can be no separate Māori government, says the PM. King Edward is king and he is represented here by his government. There can't be two suns shining in the sky at the same time. Yes, says Rua, there is only one sun in the heavens but it shines on one side – the Pākehā side.

*Maungapōhatu.*

When World War 1 comes Rua says it is wrong to fight for a Pākehā King and country because the British Crown is so unfair to Māori. Rua is arrested in 1915 for illegally selling alcohol at Maungapōhatu. You are to go before a magistrate in January 1916, he is told. I need a delay, says Rua, I'm harvesting then, I'll go next month. The magistrate says no, Rua does not turn up in January, and on a Sunday in April an armed force of 57 constables are sent secretly from Auckland and are joined by two smaller forces from Gisborne and Whakatāne. Rua is on the marae. Unarmed. Someone fires a shot, a gun battle follows. Two Māori lie dead. One is Rua's son.

The authorities take Rua up to Auckland Supreme Court. You are accused of talking against conscription of men for the war and of encouraging your followers to resist the police, Rua hears. A very long trial. The jury struggles to reach a verdict but the judge sentences Rua to a year's imprisonment with hard labour and another 18 months of 'reformative detention'. Several jury members think that is so harsh they protest in public and petition Parliament about it. Rua stays in prison until 1918.

## Mahi Skills

1. **Local history:** Explain how Tūhoe until the 1860s has little or no history with Government and from the 1860s does have history.

2. **Triple mapping:** Make maps to show the following locations: Te Urewera in New Zealand; Te Urewera in relation to Rotorua, Whakatāne, Gisborne; Ruatāhuna, Rūātoki, Lake Waikaremoana in Te Urewera.

3. **Explaining roles:** Explain the role each of the following play in helping involve Tūhoe with the Crown. *Rewi Maniapoto, Kereopa, Te Kooti, Major Rāpata Wahawaha* and *Rua Kēnana.*

4. **Comparing examples:** The MP who introduces the law about stopping tohunga practising is James Carroll, who has Ngāti Kahungunu and Irish descent. Rua Kēnana is a traditional faith healer and spiritual leader and so local police are told to watch him as he is suspected of acting as a tohunga. Explain how this is an example of different ideas being held by two people of some similar whakapapa.

5. **Perspective:** Englishman Captain Thomas Porter serves with Ngāti Porou fighting Te Kooti and is part of the force that invades Te Urewera on 6 May 1869. After he leaves the cavalry, he stays in New Zealand and marries a Ngāti Porou woman. Suggest why his perspective on government might be different to that of Rua Kēnana.

# 37 Parihaka

**Historians look at events in context. Context is the background and environment that make up the setting; it helps people understand the event better. A Māori village practising peaceful resistance to the Crown? Why? When you learn about the context – that the Crown has confiscated land from Māori that the village is on and has not given them reserves they promised – you get a fuller picture.**

*Te Whiti.*

Some Kiwis associate 5 November with Guy Fawkes trying to blow up Parliament and the King in England in 1605. Some associate it with Te Rā o te Pāhua, the Day of Plunder in 1881. This is the day when about 1600 Crown forces come to a Māori village called Parihaka led by Te Whiti, Tohu, and Tītokowaru.

Te Whiti and kinsman Tohu are of Te Āti Awa and Taranaki. Traditions say that as boys both have special gifts and go on to become prophets. When soldiers destroy Warea, where Te Whiti and Tohu go to mission school and later work, the two shift inland to Parihaka. They support the Māori king and oppose land sales. Later, Tītokowaru joins them. An organiser, he can put ideas and plans into action.

In July 1880, Government passes the Māori Prisoners Act to get rid of trials. Some MPs strongly object, but now arrested ploughmen and fencers can be kept in prison and they do not have to be given trials. In September 1880, Parliament passes the West Coast Settlements (North Island) Act, which makes some activities such as removing survey pegs, erecting fences, and ploughing, criminal offences. The British Parliament asks about rumours Māori prisoners are mistreated.

*Armed Constables ready to invade Parihaka.*

Parihaka.

Parihaka becomes a centre of non-violent resistance to Government confiscating land and not setting aside promised reserves for Māori. People wear the raukura albatross feather as a sign of peace. About 1500 people live there but others come to meetings and some stay for months at a time, swelling the population to several thousand. Other iwi send gifts of food, money, cloaks, greenstone. The village grows its food and looks after itself. It has bullocks, horses, carts, fences, police, bank, threshing and reaping machines, bakery. In March 1879 Government starts to survey confiscated land on the Waimate plain. Must be getting it ready for Pākehā, the people of Parihaka say, but not marking out the reserves promised for us. They take out surveying pegs. Miles of them. They pack up surveying camps, load everything onto carts and take them across Waingongoro River. They plough settlers' grassland. They ignore threats that they and their horses will be shot. They do not resist when troops surround and arrest them. Other ploughmen take their place. Government sends forces to build a coast road through the area. Soldiers pull Parihaka fences down. Villagers put them up again. Government arrests fencers. Other fencers take their place and put fences up again. Soldiers take them down and arrest fencers. Parihaka people are arrested and jailed in Dunedin, Lyttelton, Hokitika and Wellington.

Rumours fly in Pākehā settlements that Parihaka is arming, getting ready to invade. The *Taranaki Herald* reports Parihaka is in a horribly filthy state; a doctor visits and says it is clean, swept and has excellent drainage. An official visits Parihaka and reports large cultivations, friendly and contented inhabitants, no fortifications or military preparations. But Parihaka is sending a message; we are outside the Crown system. A tense situation.

On 5 November, Crown troops march to Parihaka, led by Native Minister John Bryce in military uniform with sabre on a white horse. Several thousand Māori sit and singing children greet the troops. One child will become the first Māori doctor and Minister of Health, Sir Māui Pōmare. A cavalry horse will shortly stand on his foot and give him a limp. Bryce orders the arrest of Parihaka leaders. Troops burn homes and crops, take away property, send away people with no money or food or shelter, set up checkpoints to stop Māori going to or from Taranaki without a pass, and ban gatherings of over 50 Māori. The Commission which later investigates is told troops rape females.

Government puts an information blackout on its actions. It takes much of the promised reserves as compensation for the cost of its military action. Tohu, Te Whiti, Tītokowaru, and Wiremu Hīroki are sent to New Plymouth. Hīroki is convicted of murdering a surveyor, and hanged. Tītokowaru is charged with using threatening language and kept for eight months. He gives up a hunger strike only when jailers say they will force-feed him. Te Whiti and Tohu are charged with encouraging people to rebel. They are held in New Plymouth for nearly six months, then sent to the South Island. In 1883 they return to Parihaka and start rebuilding.

## Mahi Skills

1 **Local history:** The history of what happens to Parihaka males is better known than the history of what happens to females. Explain why the female history is for locals to hold and share or not share.

2 **Cartoon analysis:** This cartoon appeared in 1880. State who the men and the bird represent, what the choice is, and which choice is applied to Parihaka. (Clue: Salting a bird's tail is an old belief that putting salt on the tail will make the bird unable to fly for a little while and therefore easy to capture.)

THE NEW NATIVE POLICY.

A CHOICE BETWEEN SALT AND LEAD. WHAT WILL BE THE RESULT?

3 **Mistaken ideas:** Describe how colonial authorities may think in 1881 they have broken the spirit of Māori whereas they may instead have helped to keep the ideas of Te Whiti and Tohu alive. Then work out how it might have happened that many generations of people believe the Parihaka prisoners are kept in a Dunedin cave but new research suggests that this is not true.

4 **Understanding a definition:** Many newspaper reports describe the arrested ploughmen and fencers as political prisoners – people punished for disagreeing with their Government. Consider the situation and actions of the ploughmen and fencers and state if you agree with the newspapers.

5 **Remembering through art:** Find a piece of art that is about Parihaka. Starters could be Tim Finn's *Parihaka* song, or the poem *The Charge at Parihaka* by Jessie Mackay. *The Charge at Parihaka* is a parody (a comical and exaggerated imitation of something else) of a famous 1854 poem by English poet Tennyson called *The Charge of the Light Brigade* about British soldiers charging Russian cannons during a war.


PHOTOCOPYING OF THIS PAGE IS RESTRICTED UNDER LAW.
ISBN: 9780170462419

# Ending Warfare

# 38

**Historians know that what they say may be picked over by critics and challenged. They need to choose words carefully. They might say the wars end when shots are fired at Mangaone south of Waikaremoana on 14 February 1872. That is where Te Kooti again manages to run away from his hunters in Te Urewera. However, some people will point out that the Māori King is not yet home in Waikato.**

In the King Country, King Tāwhiao continues to argue against land surveys, land sales, courts, gold-mining, telegraphs, schools and the justice system. Government wants Tāwhiao to take the oath of allegiance and open the King Country to settlement. Tāwhiao turns down offers of a pension, house, official position, return of some confiscated land. He wants Māori and Pākehā to stay separated. He wants the return of all confiscated land.

*King Tāwhiao.*

In 1881, after years of negotiation with the Crown, King Tāwhiao suggests a meeting with the Crown's representative at Alexandra (Pirongia) military post. One day in July, he and several hundred Waikato Māori, most on horses, come into Alexandra. Major William Mair, Resident Magistrate, meets them. Tāwhiao lays down his gun. Many of his men do the same. Mair accepts them. He offers to return the weapons but Tāwhiao refuses. Mair offers his own gun to Tāwhiao who accepts it. This is the end of warfare in this land, Tāwhiao says.

The Māori King is back. Tāwhiao tells Waikato, The killing of men must stop; the destruction of land must stop. I shall bury my patu in the earth and it shall not rise again ... Waikato, lie down. Do not allow blood to flow from this time on.

However, confiscated land continues to be a big issue for Kīngitanga. The catchcry is, *I riro whenua atu, me hoki whenua mai*. As land was taken then land should be given back.

In 1884 Tāwhiao leads a group to England to petition Queen Victoria. He believes Māori have a special relationship with the Queen. He wants to tell her Māori want an independent Māori parliament and an independent commission of inquiry into land confiscation. He wants to tell her that Kīngitanga is not trying to go it alone and does not reject her authority, that Māori King and British Queen can coexist in peace. Tāwhiao does not get to meet the Queen. Instead he meets Lord Derby of the Colonial Office. No longer our responsibility, Lord Derby says. Your petition must go to the New Zealand Government. Back it comes. The New Zealand Government dismisses it.

Māori keep petitioning. Government, they say, should let us share power. And take notice of our ideas about land. And how much land do Māori have a hundred years after the Treaty? Not even two million hectares out of the 26.8 million hectares. Government is still passing laws about our land, they say. Look at this Māori Affairs Act in 1953 and its later amendment (same act with changes); letting the Crown take our land it says is 'uneconomic'. Another land-grab. Does it think we have changed our minds and no longer treasure land Government says is not economic? That law comes about the same time as a reigning British sovereign visits Waitangi — a big first for history.

Queen Victoria.

## Mahi Skills

1 **Local history:** See if you can find someone in your local area who can remember the visit of Queen Elizabeth II and can tell you about it.

2 **Heeding messages:** Explain why King Tāwhiao's words to Waikato may help explain Waikato's lack of interest when Britain needs soldiers for World War 1, 1914–18.

3 **Relationship continuity and change:** Work out the difference between continuity and change and state if you can see evidence of either in the relationship between Crown and Māori.

4 **Filming:** Imagine you are making a film of the 1881 meeting. Name the music you would use as you show riders approach the military post. Say why you choose that music.

5 **Producing evidence:** Produce evidence for or against this statement: *Land and power-sharing are still controversial issues at the end of the wars.*


PHOTOCOPYING OF THIS PAGE IS RESTRICTED UNDER LAW.
ISBN: 9780170462419

# Casualties of War

39

**Historians sometimes make generalisations – broad statements that fit most events but not always all. They look at what gets lost and damaged in wars – people, land, relationships, feelings of security and belonging, belief that Government has the best interests of all its people at heart.**

How many people die in the wars? A generalisation is around 3000. Most are Māori, but how many Māori is unknown. Missionaries or soldiers who clear a field after a battle count bodies. But Māori may have taken some to bury. Some may be hidden in bush. Sometimes Māori clear the field and bury their dead and soldiers and kūpapa. European written records do not include women, children and old people. Nor others such as those who later die in prison. Some historians suggest Māori deaths should be compared to those of World War 1 which Kiwis often think of as their biggest killing-field. Historians have worked out that the Māori casualty rate of the Waikato Wars may be higher per head of population than New Zealand soldiers in World War 1.

Wars affect Pākehā and Māori children. Some lose contact with families. The generally accepted version of six-year-old Ngātau Omahuru has him in Taranaki forest on the day Crown forces and kūpapa attack Te Ngutu-o-te-manu. Kūpapa kidnap him and take him to Whanganui. Three years later, and although Ngātau Omahuru's parents are alive, William Fox, who becomes Premier of New Zealand, informally adopts him and changes his name to William Fox.

Some children are killed. A Whanganui settlement bears the name of Maxwell, a sergeant with militia there in 1868. The agreed historic account in Ngā Rauru Kītahi's Deed of Settlement with the Crown says that on 27 November 1868, a volunteer group led by John Bryce meets a group of unarmed Māori children at a woolshed. The militia fire on the group, then chase them on horseback and attack them with sabres. Two are killed and others wounded. The official report at the time praises Maxwell. In the far future Ngā Rauru and its hapū Ngāti Maika will seek a change of name for Maxwell to Pākaraka. They will also say there is a sole survivor that day of 1868 and more than two boys are killed.

Each area is affected in its own way but a generalisation is that while the physical fighting stops, for Māori the old issues of land and sovereignty and authority are still there. Tūhoe's wish to keep rangatiratanga results in a governing council of chiefs to protect the land and keep Government out. *Kaua te rori, kaua te rūri, kaua te rīhi, kaua te hoko.* No roads, no survey, no leasing land, no selling land. But there is still pressure over land. The Crown gets Tūhoe to sell land at Waikaremoana by threatening confiscation. The issues are still alive in the next century and the century after that. The Crown will set up Te Urewera National Park in the future. It will not consult Tūhoe on this.

Von Tempsky's romanticised painting of a Hauhau raid.

Another example is the Dog Tax war. Councils put a tax on dogs. Some Māori are not engaged with the cash economy and have many dogs. Unfair tax, they say. In April 1898 a group of armed Māori with Ngāpuhi prophet Hōne Tōia visit Rawene in Hokianga to oppose the tax. Government sends up troops and heavy guns, and a gunboat anchors off Rawene. The local Māori MP convinces Hōne Tōia to give it up and just in time Tōia gets a message out to call off the ambush of troops marching up. Some Māori are arrested, some get time in prison, the hapū gets a job providing railway sleepers and pays the tax.

## Mahi Skills

1. **Local history:** Prepare a piece about how your local area or a significant place in it got its name.
2. **Providing another example:** In 1874 in Taranaki, Māori kidnap an eight-year-old Pākehā girl called Caroline 'Queenie' Perret. It is thought to be utu for her father breaking a tapu. She identifies as Māori and is 60 when a Pākehā family member recognises her. Find out some details.
3. **Image analysis:** Comment on what the image above suggests about trauma that warfare might cause.
4. **Looking for connections:** State people or events to which the following are closely connected. *Deed of Settlement*; *sabres*; *Hōne Tōia*; *gunboat*; *Kaua te rori, kaua te rūri, kaua te rīhi, kaua te hoko*; *William Fox Jr*; *clearing the field.*
5. **Appropriate use of generalisations:** Just after Parihaka, G.W. Rusden publishes a book which talks about the woolshed event. Bryce and Maxwell, he says, *dashed upon women and children* and *cut them down gleefully and with ease.* Parliament debated it. Bryce sued and won as he had not personally killed and no women were involved. Comment on how generalisations can be used at the wrong time.


PHOTOCOPYING OF THIS PAGE IS RESTRICTED UNDER LAW.
ISBN: 9780170462419

# Perspectives 40

**Historians know that perspective is about a way of looking at something and that it is shaped by factors including education, culture, experiences. They know that after the wars, people have different perspectives on what should happen next.**

Who wins the wars? Historians tend not to talk about winners and losers because even the so-called 'sides' fighting are fluid. Instead, they talk of individual engagements and look at what happens when fighting stops.

Generally a Pākehā perspective is that the Crown's ideas about the Treaty of Waitangi are going to be followed rather than Māori ideas. That means British-style groups such as Parliament, Governor, military, law courts and police rather than partnership and talks with hapū and iwi governed by rangatira. Although some Pākehā speak te reo Māori, the Pākehā perspective is that English will be the main language. The 1867 Native Schools Act which provides for Māori schools says teaching will be in English, books and stories will be in English, and although some teachers have Māori helpers, most teachers are Pākehā.

Some Māori parents think children are better off speaking English. Some children will be punished for speaking te reo Māori at school. Any history mentioned will be that of Britain and elsewhere rather than that of New Zealand, the wars or local history. This policy is assimilation – the process by which one group is absorbed into the culture of the group with the most power.

*The Native Schools Act continues the British-style education begun by missionaries.*

 PHOTOCOPYING OF THIS PAGE IS RESTRICTED UNDER LAW. 

*Land continues to be central to iwi and hapū identity. In the 1880s Te Heuheu Tūkino IV, chief of Ngāti Tuwharetoa iwi around Tongariro, is concerned settlers will take iwi land. He signs a deed with Government to make sure the sacred summits of Tongariro, Ruapehu and Ngauruhoe are never sold. This sets up a special relationship among Māori, Pākeha and land where Māori and Pākehā have the responsibility to protect the land. Tongariro becomes the first national park in the world said to be 'gifted' by indigenous people.*

A Māori perspective is that the wars never end because fighting over land and te tino rangatiratanga sovereignty will just shift into the law courts and Parliament. Iwi realise they share grievances against the Crown. Details are special to each iwi but a theme is the wish for the Crown to start honouring the Treaty and treat its Treaty partner as an equal. In the 1850s some Māori met to talk about issues such as land alienation and not having a say in laws, and in 1860 the Governor invited about 200 Māori leaders to a three-week conference at a mission station at Mission Bay in Auckland. He wanted to get Māori loyalty to the Crown and stop chiefs joining Kīngitanga. It ended with the Kohimarama Covenant which rangatira see as recognition of their mana and authority and a sign they will take part in decision-making. The Governor agreed to their request for an annual conference but held no more and now some Māori try to get Government to start up the conference again. They take petitions about honouring the Treaty to Government, travel to Britain to present petitions. Māori MPs take a formal request to Parliament. Get rid of the Native Land Court. Give Māori the right to deal with their own land. When this is read out, all non-Māori MPs walk out. And not all court cases work out as expected. An extreme example is a court case of 1877 involving Wiremu Parata, a politician of Māori and Pākehā descent who says Pākehā are making laws for Māori without understanding Māori, and Chief Justice Prendergast who says that the Treaty of Waitangi is worthless because it is signed between 'a civilised nation and a group of savages' who were not capable of signing a treaty, that the Crown's sovereignty comes from 'discovery and occupation' rather than the Treaty. Not all Pākehā agree with him.

MP Hirini Taiwhanga is becoming a bit of a nuisance to officials. He talks to iwi about how bad some government policies are. In 1882 he takes a petition to London asking for a Royal Commission to investigate and fix laws that breach the Treaty and to let a Māori Government be created to stop the New Zealand Government trying to ignore the Treaty. No meeting with Queen Victoria but the group do get to meet the Secretary of State for the Colonies. No help there. He says he has no responsibility for alleged Treaty breaches.

Māori now set up their own rangatiratanga organisations. To add to Kīngitanga, to get more political power. They hold the first Māori parliament in 1879 in the Kohimarama house. In 1881 they open a meeting house Te Tiriti o Waitangi at Te Tii marae to host other parliaments. To get a united voice in the Wellington parliament they create Te Kotahitanga o te Tiriti o Waitangi; the Wellington parliament ignores it. Kīngitanga sets up a parliament, Te Kauhanganui, in 1890; it tries but fails to join up with Kotahitanga.


PHOTOCOPYING OF THIS PAGE IS RESTRICTED UNDER LAW.
ISBN: 9780170462419

The religious movement Rātana is founded at the end of World War 1 by faith healer Tahupōtiki Wiremu Rātana. It has a political wing and works to get the return of confiscated lands, to get the Crown to honour the Treaty. Rātana and a group take a petition to London in 1924. One group member tries, but fails, to present the petition to the League of Nations, the forerunner of the United Nations, in Geneva. In 1936 Rātana meets with Labour Prime Minister Michael Savage. He gives him five objects. A Rātana badge symbolises Rātana's followers who will support Savage if he does something to put Māori on a more equal footing to Pākehā. A pounamu hei tiki symbolises Māori mana which is threatened. Huia feathers symbolise Māori – huia birds are extinct, their feathers are taonga. A kūmara symbolises Māori lack of land to grow food. A broken watch, belonging to Rātana's grandfather, symbolises poverty because grandfather had and grandson has no money to get it fixed.

In 1909 the Young Māori Party is formed. Not an official political party; a group that begins as former students from Te Aute College in Hawke's Bay. They want to improve Māori lives and generally think that European-style education and health services will be helpful. Some leading people are Apirana Ngata, Te Rangi Hīroa (Peter Buck), James Carroll, Māui Pōmare.

In 1951 Te Rōpū Wāhine Māori, Māori Women's Welfare League, is set up to help Māori women and whānau. Government supports it so it may be a way to get access to Government officials; it gets involved in political issues such as housing, education, health.

Decolonisation becomes a big word. Means the unbundling of colonisation, freeing colonised people from colonial laws and policies that alienate them from traditions. Respected Māori lawyer Moana Jackson talks about alternatives to prison. No such word in traditional Māori society, he says. Maybe, he says, New Zealand's criminal justice system could go back to restoring relationships between offenders and victims and getting balance. It worked for Māori for centuries.

## Mahi Skills

1 **Local history:** Outline some ways people in local areas might get involved in Māori efforts to get their voices heard.

2 **Understanding assimilation:** Explain why the expectation for laws and policies is that Māori are absorbed into Pākehā organisation and government and not vice versa.

3 **Linking perspective with action:** Show by using examples how having perspectives on government and organisation can lead to actions.

4 **Understanding exceptions:** Think about generalisations and explain how talking about a Pākehā perspective or a Māori perspective does not mean every Pākehā or Māori has those perspectives.

5 **Learning history:** After the wars, European settlers keep arriving in New Zealand. Comment on how much knowledge of New Zealand history they are likely to bring with them and learn in their new country.

# 41 Economic Organisation

**Historians know that every place where there are people has some sort of economy – the way people produce and consume goods (such as food) and services (such as delivering food). Historians look at the effect that events such as wars have on the economy.**

The wars help cement in place a Pākehā-type economy with features including money, banks, buying and selling, individual ownership, clearing land for big sheep stations and smaller dairy farms, gold-mining and international trading.

*When the Operiki settlement upriver from Whanganui is rebuilt nearby on better land, it is renamed Koriniti by a missionary.*

*Although Māori have a long history of settlements around Ōtepoti, it gets named Dunedin after the Scottish Gaelic name for Edinburgh.*

Alienation of Māori land stops many hapū and iwi being able to produce. An endless circle of poor diet and poor living conditions makes for poor health. The Māori population nose-dives which causes Pākehā to talk of needing to smooth down the dying pillow of the Māori race. Government makes some efforts to help Māori farming. For example, it gives young mulberries and silkworms to iwi along Whanganui River although there seem to be no records of silk being produced. There is mention in Parliament that help has been given, including tools and machinery, seeds and financial help to get flour mills, to *the defeated tribes* to get a farming economy running. Some younger Māori work for wages on buildings such as roads and railways, clearing bush, shearing, harvesting and digging for kauri gum.


PHOTOCOPYING OF THIS PAGE IS RESTRICTED UNDER LAW.
ISBN: 9780170462419

*Although Māori have a long history of settlements around Whakaraupō, it gets named Lyttelton after a British MP.*

*Native Land Court continues its work; here at Ōhinemutu.*

## Mahi Skills

1 **Local history:** Find out what you can of your area's economic history.

2 **Understanding economic organisation:** Show how conflict can impact on economic organisation.

3 **Locating and quoting:** Find and quote the sentence in this chapter that best matches the following.

> The wife of New Zealand's first Chief Justice travels in Waikato in 1852 and later says, *We little dreamed that in ten years the peaceful industry of the whole district would cease and the land become a desert through our unhappy war.*

4 **Inferring (using evidence to understand):** State what inferences you get from the images.

5 **Oral discourse:** Comment about how comfortable you would feel spending time talking about this topic in a group discussion.

# 42 Healing Relationships

**Historians know that conflict, whether caused by wars, laws or policies, can cause broken hearts and broken relationships. One broken relationship is the Crown-Māori one. After the Treaty signing, a hundred years before the United Nations' Universal Declaration of Human Rights arrives in the world, Māori start looking to get human rights through dialogue and a changed relationship with the Crown and after the wars they continue to do so.**

In 1975 Government passes the Treaty of Waitangi Act to create a Waitangi Tribunal. Its job is to investigate Treaty breaches by the Crown. Two large claims get settled before the end of the century. Each for about $170 million. The Waikato-Tainui Settlement includes cash payment, return of some land, formal apology from the Crown. The Ngāi Tahu Settlement includes cash payment, return of ancestral maunga Aoraki, formal apology from the Crown.

At Tribunal hearings, historians present histories which include the wars. For example, the Tribunal finds the Crown was justified in military action in 1869 to find Te Kooti when he hid in Te Urewera. It says Māori also breached Treaty responsibilities as citizens and Treaty partners, that there was no justification for the murder of Pākehā settlers and other Māori in the Tūranga area by Te Kooti and his followers. It says the Crown repeatedly disregarded its own laws in its treatment of Māori from the Tūranga area, including deporting and detaining 123 prisoners on Wharekauri without charge or trial, and executing unarmed prisoners at Ngātapa pā in 1868 without charge or trial.

*Unlike Britain, the New Zealand Parliament has no Upper House, although this cartoon suggests the Tribunal has a lot of power.*

The Tribunal can also look at the Treaty itself, and the 1835 He Whakaputanga Declaration of Independence. An example is the Tribunal's Te Paparahi o Te Raki (Great Land of the North) Inquiry which is in two stages. Stage 1 is about the meaning and effect of the Treaty, the expectation of chiefs when they sign, what Ngāpuhi rangatira agree to, whether they sign away their sovereignty or the right to make their own laws.


PHOTOCOPYING OF THIS PAGE IS RESTRICTED UNDER LAW.
ISBN: 9780170462419

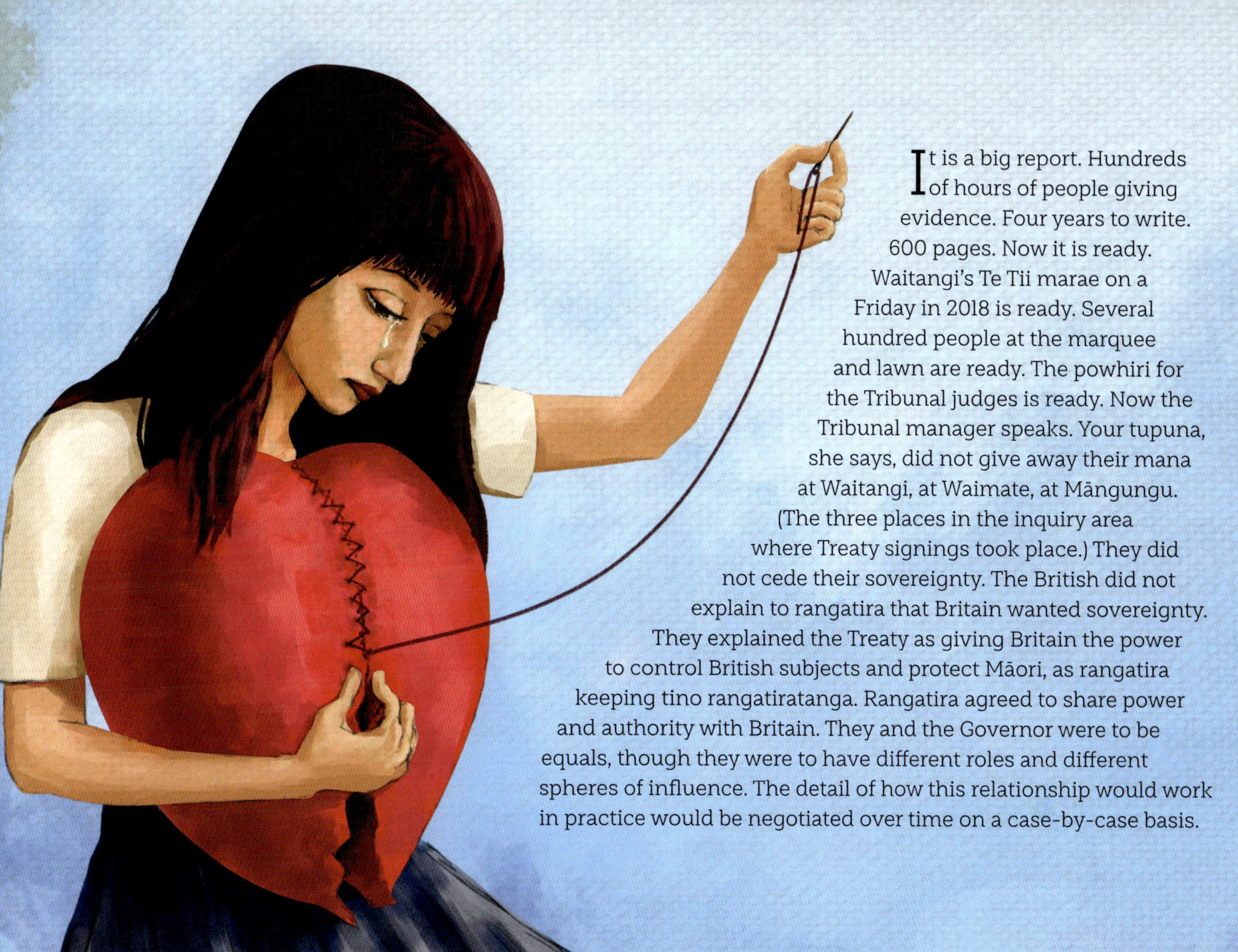

It is a big report. Hundreds of hours of people giving evidence. Four years to write. 600 pages. Now it is ready. Waitangi's Te Tii marae on a Friday in 2018 is ready. Several hundred people at the marquee and lawn are ready. The powhiri for the Tribunal judges is ready. Now the Tribunal manager speaks. Your tupuna, she says, did not give away their mana at Waitangi, at Waimate, at Māngungu. (The three places in the inquiry area where Treaty signings took place.) They did not cede their sovereignty. The British did not explain to rangatira that Britain wanted sovereignty. They explained the Treaty as giving Britain the power to control British subjects and protect Māori, as rangatira keeping tino rangatiratanga. Rangatira agreed to share power and authority with Britain. They and the Governor were to be equals, though they were to have different roles and different spheres of influence. The detail of how this relationship would work in practice would be negotiated over time on a case-by-case basis.

What does the Crown think of this message? Tribunal findings are not binding. Government does not have act on them. The Treaty Settlements Minister says there is no question the Crown has sovereignty in New Zealand and the report does not change that.

History is all about people. Think of two people as examples. Here is William Hobson on the evening of 5 February 1840. He is walking down from Busby's place to the beach where a boat waits to row him out to his anchored ship. He is not well, does not speak or read te reo Māori, is doing his job as best as he can; now he is talking to missionary Colenso about printing the Treaty which he believes will give Britain sovereignty in New Zealand. Just as he gets to the boat, an elderly Māori man hurries up to him. Stares at him, says, *Auee! He koroheke! Ekore e roa kua mate.* Hobson asks Colenso, What did he say? Colenso tries to shrug it off. Tell me the truth, insists Hobson. And so Colenso says, *Alas! An old man! He will soon be dead.* Two years later, at 50 years old, Hobson has another stroke and dies. Still believing British have sovereignty.

And here is Hōne Heke, the first chief to sign the Treaty on 6 February 1840. Two years after Hobson dies, Heke is organising the symbol of British sovereignty to be chopped down and then he is fighting a war. During a battle he hears his ally Te Kākaha is mortally wounded. He goes to help and gets wounded himself. He is ill for some time but keeps fighting through letters to governors and missionaries. In 1850, not yet 50 years old, he dies of tuberculosis. Still insisting that Māori never gave up tino rangatiratanga.

In 2015 a hapū leader and a lawyer argue over oral history versus written history in a New Plymouth court. Greymouth Petroleum wants to dig a well site in Waitara Valley. Wiremu Kīngi Te Rangitāke is buried in the area, says Otaraua hapū, supported by Pukerangiora hapū. Why can't you say exactly where? the lawyer asks. That would break a promise given to my grandfather the day before he died, the hapū chairman answers. He pointed out the site, told me to look out for it and swore me to secrecy. There is no historical record of Wiremu Kīngi

ISBN: 9780170462419 PHOTOCOPYING OF THIS PAGE IS RESTRICTED UNDER LAW. 

being buried in the area, says the lawyer. Counsel has no right, says the hapū chairman, to suggest my record of events is any less correct than that captured in the Pākehā history books which he relies on. Another dispute is whether the remains of people killed in the Pukerangiora pā sacking are in the proposed well area. A Pukerangiora kuia supports the statement that Wiremu Kīngi and Pukerangiora victims are buried in the area as her grandfather had told her in Māori, and she knows the sacredness of the whole area.

Iwi try to heal a relationship with another iwi. For example, in 2013 Tūhoe, at a tangi, give a peace gift to Ngāti Porou. This is to end nearly 150 years of division. The Crown tries to heal a relationship with individuals and their ancestors. For example, descendants of Mokomoko say he claimed he went away after the decision to kill Völkner was made, and he had earlier tried to help Völkner escape. The Justice Minister visits Ōpōtiki in 1993 to apologise to Te Whakatōhea and Mokomoko descendants and overturn the conviction. He does this without consulting te whānau a Mokomoko. The pardon differs to that of two Ngāti Awa for the same event. Te whānau a Mokomoko are concerned that the Mokomoko pardon does not restore his character, mana and reputation or those of his descendants. In 2011 they sign a pardon agreement with the Crown.

The Crown tries to heal a relationship with communities. For example, 136 years after Crown troops invade Parihaka, the Crown goes in peace to the village. He Puanga Haeata, the Parihaka-Crown ceremony, takes place on Friday, 9 June 2017. Haeata means dawn; so a new beginning. The Treaty Negotiations Minister delivers an apology to Parihaka on behalf of the Crown. The Crown tries to heal a relationship with a group. For example, the Crown acknowledges it acted unjustly and in breach of the Treaty of Waitangi in its dealings with Kīngitanga and Waikato in sending its forces across the Mangatāwhiri in July 1863 and in unfairly labelling Waikato as rebels. It apologises for the loss of lives, ruin of property and social life, confiscations of land and resources, feelings of grief and being orphaned that its actions caused.

## Mahi Skills

1 **Local history:** Check to see if your local area has been involved in a Waitangi Tribunal inquiry and explain why it has been or has not been.

2 **Recognising oral and written sources:** State if you think both should be acceptable in a law court and why you think that.

3 **Looking to the future:** Show in any format your idea about a possible future of New Zealand. Use your knowledge of the New Zealand Wars and think how knowing about the past can help shape the future.

4 **Getting the message:** State what message you think the cartoonist is sending in this cartoon and how he does it. Then do the same for the cartoon on page 116.

5 **Understanding reconciliation:** Give examples of reconciliation – trying to restore balance and respect in a relationship.

PHOTOCOPYING OF THIS PAGE IS RESTRICTED UNDER LAW.
ISBN: 9780170462419

# Trying to Re-Treat

# 43

**Historians understand that some people talk about the negotiations of 1840 around the Treaty of Waitangi as treating. When Māori start asking to renegotiate with the Crown to get more rangatiratanga, they are trying to re-treat and the young Māori who lead this are known as the rangatiratanga generations. Historians understand the need for Crown and Māori to listen to each other's stories with respect. They look at ways the group without rangatiratanga power, Māori, try to get the group with sovereignty power, the Crown, to listen, and then act.**

Some Māori try symbolic actions. Looking back to Heke and the flagpole. The Māori Sovereignty Liberation Organisation claims responsibility for an attack on the America's Cup; the man who smashes into it with a sledgehammer says the Cup is a symbol of oppression and none of the money from racing the Cup will reach Māori. An attack on the pine tree on One Tree Hill on the anniversary of the signing of the Declaration of Independence is to protest Government putting a money limit on Treaty claims. A man takes a Colin McCahon triptych, said to be a visual short history of Tūhoe, from Lake Waikaremoana's Visitor Centre; he returns the painting the following year and says he wanted people to feel what it is like to have treasure taken off them forcibly. A Māori student throws a wet T-shirt at Queen Elizabeth during the 150th Treaty commemoration; she says she is protesting 150 years of bad treatment of Māori. The T-shirt misses the sovereign and lands on the car she is in. The student gets several months of periodic detention.

*Whina Cooper leads hīkoi.*

Some Māori try marching. In 1975, 79-year-old Whina Cooper leads a hīkoi march from the Far North to Parliament in Wellington and gives a Memorial of Rights calling for not one more acre of Māori land to be taken. A group of marchers stay and set up a Tent Embassy on Parliament Grounds.

Some Māori try protesting. Ngā Tamatoa (The Warriors) calls for the Crown to honour the Treaty, to get te reo Māori taught in schools. It begins a history of protests at Waitangi Day ceremonies by one year wearing black armbands to show mourning for alienated Māori land. The newly formed Māori political party Mana Motuhake wants Māori authority and power; the Māori Party founded in 2004 wants to work for Māori within Parliament and the Government.

Some Māori try occupations on disputed land. A group occupies Takahue School in the Far North because it is on land that they say should be returned to Māori as the Government deal that bought it in 1875 is unsound. When Government announces a housing development on former Ngāti Whātua reserve land at Bastion Point Takaparawhā in Auckland, a group occupies the land; after 506 days Government sends in police to evict them. After a Waitangi Tribunal inquiry much of the land is returned.

During World War II Government takes Māori land at Raglan Whāingaroa for an emergency military airfield and displaces people from homes which it destroys. The airfield is not needed and the land is not returned; part of it is turned into a golf course. A protest to get it back includes fencing off the urupā on the golf course and inviting tohunga and supporters from outside to gather there for a ceremony on the day of the golf course's annual tournament. Some are arrested for trespass. When the Crown finally withdraws its demand of payment for the land, the land is vested in Te Kopua Trust.

Some Māori look to the United Nations for help. In 2016 a spokesperson for the Indigenous Peoples of Aotearoa takes an appeal to the United Nations for Māori to get their tino rangatiratanga recognised and acknowledged. The appeal lists grievances against the Crown such as its failure to consult with Māori, and charges it with genocide and discrimination against Māori.

When Government and Council designate 32 hectares next to Otuataua Stonefields Historic Reserve for housing, SOUL (Save Our Unique Landscape) gets involved. This Ihumātao block of land on the shores of Manukau Harbour is believed to be the first place where Māori in Tāmaki Makaurau Auckland settled and gardened. Confiscated during the Crown invasion of Waikato, sold to a private owner, now owned by a Fletcher Building company. An occupation of the land begins. In 2017 two people fly to New York to talk to the United Nations about the situation in the hope it will make Government and Council start listening. A hīkoi to Parliament asks Government to stop a confrontation at Ihumātao, another hīkoi delivers a petition to the Auckland mayor calling for Council and Government to protect the land. An eviction notice is served to occupiers, three are arrested, the Māori King visits, Government Ministers visit, more police arrive, protests take place around the country and in 2020 Government agrees to buy the land. A Memorandum of Understanding (He Pūmautanga) is signed by Kīngitanga, Crown and Auckland Council which sets out how parties will work together to decide the future of the land.

Working together becomes a key phrase. A United Nations committee says Government should act on Tribunal recommendations. The UN also tells Government, You did not consult properly with Māori over Ihumātao. You are supposed to get their consent before you sign off any project that will affect their traditional land and resources.


PHOTOCOPYING OF THIS PAGE IS RESTRICTED UNDER LAW.
ISBN: 9780170462419

## Mahi Skills

1 **Local history:** Identify the tino rangatiratanga flag. Say if you have seen it around your local area.

2 **Preparing a case study:** A case study is an in-depth look at one event which will help understanding of a general theme. Choose an event mentioned in this chapter or another protest and prepare a case study on it. Try to include mention of how and why some non-Māori support the event.

3 **Understanding category:** Describe how Māori actions to try to re-treat and renegotiate with the Crown can be categorised as being alongside or inside or outside Government.

4 **Supplying examples:** State the difference between action at a local level, action at a national level, and action at an international level and give examples for each level.

5 **Analysing a cartoon:** Prepare notes to share about the Ihumātao cartoon. Think about features you can observe and ideas you can infer.

# 44 Remembering

**Historians look at ways people record and remember the past. They know that things like statues and plaques put up to honour the dead in the New Zealand Wars and names of places become more than memorials and names because politics gets involved in their going-up and coming-down.**

Just before Covid-19 starts a global pandemic, New Zealand holds its first He Rā Maumahara National Day of commemoration for the New Zealand Wars. It takes place on 11 March 2018, the anniversary of the sacking of Kororāreka. The date 28 October is nominated as future annual days of remembrance for stories about the wars to be role-played, shared, remembered and talked about. Around the same time a plaque for the wars is unveiled in Parliament. Parliament's Tumu Whakarae (Chief Executive) says it is a reminder of those who were lost to the war and also for the desire to unify and heal both land and people.

Few memorials go up straight after the wars. Iwi and hapū keep their histories; maybe a child is given a special name. Pākehā are not keen to commemorate battles imperial soldiers fought; maybe there are other battles they want to forget. There are a few exceptions, including the pyramid in Tuamarina cemetery to the memory of settlers who died in the Wairau Affray, and the church Māori build near Ōhaeawai as a symbol of peace and tribute to Pākehā who died in that battle.

On 1 April 1914, several thousand gather on the site of the Ōrākau battle. Kids in Waikato and Waipa get a holiday, and schools that cannot get to the site are to hold an assembly, raise the flag and give a lesson on *the difficulties of early settlement in New Zealand*. Newspapers report on the noble spirit, heroic defence and courage of Ōrākau warriors. Is this Pākehā taking over a Māori story, some ask, to get people to feel good about their country while forgetting Māori might not think Ōrākau is something to celebrate? The event happens shortly before World War 1 starts, and at the time of a hui at Waahi about the upcoming trip of the Māori King to Britain with a petition about the Treaty partner.

A century later, on 21 February, a plaque is unveiled at dawn on the site of Rangiaowhia where local iwi think whare stood before they burned. It says *Ko tēnei kōwhatu hei whakamaumaharatanga i te pāhautanga i pā ki runga i a Ngāti Apakura, Ngāti Hinetū me ngā iwi ki konei ki Rangiaowhia i te 21 o Pēpuere, 1864*. This stone is a memorial to the atrocities suffered by Ngāti Apakura, Ngāti Hinetū and others here at Rangiaowhia on the 21st of February, 1864. A Māori historian and a Pākehā historian give speeches at the unveiling.


PHOTOCOPYING OF THIS PAGE IS RESTRICTED UNDER LAW.
ISBN: 9780170462419

Many memorials are controversial. Some use expressions such as in defence of law and order against fanaticism and barbarism, a brave soldier and staunch ally of the New Zealand Government during the troublous times of the Māori rebellion against British authority. A businessman gives Hamilton a statue of Captain Hamilton who died of wounds he got at Gate Pā; Waikato-Tainui asks for its removal and later it is splattered with red paint. In 2020 the city council removes the statue. To many settlers Bryce is Honest John; to many Māori he is Tangata Kōhuru — Murderous Man. Streets and roads get his name, along with others such as Cameron, Chute, Von Tempsky, Grey. Some Māori and Pākehā ask for them to be renamed.

On 16 June 2002 a Katikara memorial is unveiled on the site of an old redoubt that marks the mass grave of more than 20 Māori killed on 4 June 1863 in an attack by a Crown force supported by artillery from a steamship where Governor Grey watches. The memorial is a partnership between local hapū and the Ministry for Culture and Heritage.

On 18 December 2017 Dutch officials meet descendants from Mohua who present a pounamu stone as a reconciliation gift. In 2019 New Zealand commemorates the 250th anniversary of Captain Cook's visit. Some are proud of their heritage and want to celebrate Cook. The four Gisborne iwi refuse to hold a pōwhiri. Cook is a murderer, some say, the reason why land is taken, the introducer of diseases, the cause of colonisation. The British High Commissioner meets with local iwi. She says, *I acknowledge the deaths of nine of your ancestors ... who were killed by the crew of the* Endeavour.

# Mahi Skills

1 **Local history:** Check if any memorials mark local involvement in a historical event. If there is no memorial, choose one from somewhere else. Describe the memorial and show how it is specific to local history.

2 **Testing yourself:** Work out why 28 October is chosen for He Rā Maumahara National Day of commemoration. Check to see if your answer is correct and make a note of how well you do.

3 **Understanding appropriation:** Appropriation is taking for your own use, often without permission. Explain how it might lead to accusations of cultural insensitivity and why all cultures in a democracy are expected to be culturally sensitive.

4 **Arguments:** All around the world, people argue about memorials that commemorate certain people and events. Present as many arguments as you can for and against removing some memorials.

5 **Remembering and recording:** Make a list of ways people remember and record the past.

PHOTOCOPYING OF THIS PAGE IS RESTRICTED UNDER LAW.
ISBN: 9780170462419

# Word List

**Act** law passed by Parliament
**adultery** cheating on marriage partner
**ākonga** student
**alienation** land got from customary owners
**allegedly** claimed to have happened
**amalgamate** combine, unite with
**amazon** legendary female warrior
**analysis** detailed examination
**ancestor** relative earlier than grandparent
**apostle** person sent on mission
**arbitrary** random
**arthritis** joint pain and swelling
**assess** estimate, calculate
**assimilation** dominant culture absorbs minority
**atrocity** wicked or cruel act
**attitude** feeling or opinion
**atua** god, supernatural being
**authority** power to give orders, decide
**banditti** robbers belonging to a gang
**baptised** in Christian ceremony, christened
**barbarism** extreme cruelty or ignorance
**barracks** places to house soldiers
**barter** swap goods and services for other ones
**blockade** seal off a place
**bombarding** attacking non-stop
**booty** goods stolen in war
**breach** breaking, ignoring rule or law
**breeches** knee-length trousers
**brig** two-masted sailing ship
**bunker** underground shelter
**calabash** water container, gourd
**cannibalism** eating flesh of own species
**cannon** large heavy gun usually on wheels
**cartouche box** carries soldier's cartridges
**chain mail** armour made of small metal rings
**cholera** disease, usually from infected water
**closet** small room, toilet
**code of conduct** set of rules for group
**colonisation** taking control over indigenous people
**Commander-in-Chief** overall command of armed force
**commemoration** official remembrance and respect
**commission** group appointed to do special job
**commissioner** government official
**communal** belonging to everyone in group
**compensation** given in recognition of loss, suffering
**complex** having many parts, not easy
**confederation** union of groups or people
**confiscation** taking property away from owners
**conscription** compulsory service in armed force
**constitution** system for how country is governed
**consul** official appointed to another country
**consumer** person who uses something
**contingent** group of soldiers from elsewhere
**continuous** without interruption
**contract** agreement
**controversial** causing public disagreement
**convert** change one's religion or belief
**convict** someone in prison
**court martial** trial for breaking military law
**covenant** agreement
**covet** want something someone else has
**Crown** government of country with monarch as head
**curfew** people to stay inside at set time
**customary rights** uses according to tikanga
**defiance** open resistance
**discrimination** unfair treatment of group of people
**dispute** argument, disagreement
**dray** cart for heavy loads
**environment** surroundings
**evict** force someone to leave place
**fanaticism** extreme, unquestioning devotion
**fertile** good for growing things
**feud** long and bitter disagreement
**fiend** devil
**forbearance** patience and self-control
**forfeit** losing something as punishment
**frigate** warship
**garrison** military post
**genocide** destroying particular group
**gout** painful inflammatory arthritis disease
**governing** running a country
**Governor** official appointed to govern a place
**graphic novel** novel in comic-book style
**grievances** complaints of unfairness
**guerrilla** small army of irregular fighters
**He Ao! He Aotearoa!** A cloud! A long white cloud!
**holocaust** mass slaughter
**howitzer** cannon firing shells at high angle
**hui** meeting, gathering
**illiterate** unable to read or write
**immoral** evil
**ingenious** clever
**kai** food
**kaiako** feeder of knowledge, teacher
**kaimoana** food from sea
**karakia** prayer, chant
**kāwanatanga** governing
**Kīngitanga** Māori King Movement
**kōrero** conversation
**kōrero pūrākau** storytelling

**legend** traditional story, not proven
**loot** items taken from enemy
**magistrate** official who enforces law
**mana Māori** Māori authority, power
**mana whenua** historic authority over area
**manuhiri** visitor
**Māori** person, from māori meaning normal
**matagouri** New Zealand thorny bush
**mātauranga Māori** traditional Māori knowledge
**mediator** helps get peace between parties
**memorandum** written document
**memorial** structure to remember event, person
**mere** short, broad weapon
**migration** movement from one region to another
**mihi** greeting, welcome
**mobile** able to move or be moved
**monarch** sovereign head of state, e.g. queen
**morale** confidence when faced with hardship
**mortally** in way that causes death
**mortar** gun firing shells (bombs)
**MPs** Members of Parliament
**musket** long gun loaded from muzzle (end)
**mutineer** someone who refuses to obey orders
**mystical** magical, mysterious, supernatural
**navigator** guides vessel
**nuclear family** couple and their children
**null and void** having no legal force
**ochre** coloured earth
**occupy** enter to take control
**oppression** unjust treatment
**oral** spoken
**organisation** arrangement, particular system
**outpost** position away from main army
**outrigger** structure fixed parallel to vessel
**Pākehā** non-Māori
**palisade** fence of stakes
**patron** supports person, cause, group
**patu** stone, wooden, bone club
**patupaiarehe** fairylike supernatural beings
**perspective** point of view
**petition** formal written request
**petulance** impatient annoyance
**pike** long sharp stick weapon
**plaque** memorial on flat metal or wood
**plunder** goods got violently or dishonestly
**Pope** head of Roman Catholic Church
**pounamu** greenstone, jade
**pound** unit of money
**pōwhiri** welcoming ceremony
**prestige** respect, mana
**proclaim** announce officially
**prophet** gifted teacher
**prudently** showing care and thought
**puna** pool, spring of water
**pyre** pile on which to burn a body
**ramrod** rod to ram in charge of a musket
**rangatiritanga** independence, Māori ruling themselves
**ransack** search place for things to steal
**raupatu** confiscation of land
**ravage** cause great damage
**recital** saying out loud from memory
**reconciliation** restoring friendly relations
**redoubt** military fort for shelter
**reformative** changing to a better state
**refuge** shelter, safety
**refugee** someone forced to flee for **refuge** (safety)
**renegotiate** negotiate again to get improvement
**reserves** land set aside by government for Māori
**Resident** official representative
**resources** useful, valuable things
**Ringatū** upraised hand, Te Kooti's religion
**ritual** actions done in particular order
**rohe** border, boundary, territory
**rote learning** memorising by repetition
**rūnanga** assembly, council
**sabotage** destroying, damaging
**sabre** sword
**sack** loot a captured place
**sensational** causing public excitement
**settlement** official agreement to resolve dispute
**siege** being surrounded by enemy forces
**sovereign** supreme ruler
**sovereignty** power to make law
**spar** thick pole used for ship's mast
**spiritual** to do with soul rather than body
**steerage** lower ship deck, cheapest beds
**surveyor** measures and describes land
**sustainability** looking after resources
**swear allegiance** promise to be loyal
**symbolic** representing something
**taiaha** long wooden weapon
**tamariki** children
**tangata whenua** people of the land
**tangi** traditional Māori funeral
**taonga** something treasured
**taonga tuku iho** heirloom, heritage
**tension** emotional or mental strain
**te reo Māori** Māori language
**Te Riri Pākehā** White Man's Anger
**theodolite** surveying instrument
**theory** idea intended to explain something
**tino rangatiratanga** absolute sovereignty
**tohunga** learned person, expert, priest
**tohunga whakairo** carving expert
**tradition** customs passed down
**transportation** shipping of convicts to penal colony
**treason** betraying your country
**treaty** agreement
**tribe of Marion** French people
**tribunal** special court
**tukutuku** ornamental weaving
**tutu** extremely poisonous plant
**urupā** burial place
**wāhi tapu** sacred place
**waiata** song
**waka** canoe
**wanton** without pity
**whakapapa** genealogy
**whakataukī** proverb, saying
**whanaungatanga** kinship
**whare** house, hut
**whenua** land, placenta


PHOTOCOPYING OF THIS PAGE IS RESTRICTED UNDER LAW.
ISBN: 9780170462419

# Place List

(N.I. = North Island; S.I. = South Island)

**Akaroa** Banks Peninsula S.I.
**Arahura** west coast by Hokitika S.I.
**Arctic, Antarctic** has North & South Poles
**Bastion Point** Takaparawhā Auckland
**Battle Hill** north of Wellington N.I.
**Bay of Islands** northeast harbour N.I.
**Bay of Plenty** eastern N.I.
**Boulcott's** settler's farm at Hutt River lower N.I.
**Britain** Great Britain (Scotland Wales England)
**Britomart** Te Rerenga Ora Iti Auckland
**Burmese** to do with Burma/Myanmar
**Camp Waihi** colonial redoubt Taranaki N.I.
**Camp Waitara** on disputed land Taranaki N.I.
**Cape Town** South Africa port
**Christchurch** Canterbury S.I.
**Cloudy Bay** has Wairau R delta top of S.I.
**Colonial Office** British govt dept London
**Doubtless Bay** Northland N.I.
**Dunedin** Otago S.I.
**Dutch** to do with Netherlands/Holland
**East Coast** easternmost N.I.
**England** country of Britain
**Far North** northernmost part N.I.
**Fiordland** southwest S.I.
**Gate Pā** Pukehinahina Tauranga N.I.
**Geneva** city Switzerland
**Great South Road** Auckland/Waikato N.I.
**Hairini** ridge near Rangiaowhia Waikato N.I.
**Hamilton** by Waikato River N.I.
**Hawke's Bay** east coast N.I.
**Heretaunga** Upper Hutt by Wellington N.I.
**Hohi** cove at Rangihoua Bay of Islands N.I.
**Hokianga** area & harbour Far North N.I.
**Hokitika** west coast S.I.
**House of Lords** Upper House British Parliament
**Howick** Auckland N.I.
**Hui Te Rangiora** iwi council-house Waikato N.I.
**Ihumātao** Auckland N.I.
**Ireland** all one country at this time with Britain
**Kaiapoi** Canterbury S.I.
**Kaikōura** east coast north of Christchurch S.I.
**Kaimanawa** mountains central N.I.
**Kaipopo** pā near New Plymouth N.I.
**Kākāpō Bay** Marlborough S.I.
**Katikara** near New Plymouth N.I.
**Kawakawa** Bay of Islands N.I.
**Kawhia** west coast Waikato N.I.
**Kerikeri** Northland N.I.
**Ketemarae** Taranaki N.I.
**Kihikihi** Waikato N.I.
**King Country** eastern mid N.I.
**Koheroa** south of Queen's redoubt Waikato N.I.
**Kohimarama** Auckland N.I.
**Koroniti** upriver from Whanganui N.I.
**Kororāreka** Russell Bay of Islands N.I.
**Lake Ngaroto** Waikato N.I.
**Lake Ōmāpere** Northland N.I.
**Lake Waikaremoana** Te Urewera N.I.
**Lake Wakatipu** near Queenstown S.I.
**Lichfield** cathedral city England
**London** England has British parliament
**Lyttelton** east coast near Christchurch S.I.
**Maketu** coast Bay of Plenty N.I.
**Mangaohoi** stream near Te Awamutu N.I.
**Mangaone** near southeast corner N.I.
**Mangapiko** Waipa tributary Waikato N.I.
**Mangapōhatu** Te Urewera N.I.
**Mangatāwhiri** Waikato tributary N.I.
**Māngere** Auckland N.I.
**Mangonui** Northland N.I.
**Māngungu** Hokianga harbour N.I.
**Manukau** harbour Auckland N.I.
**Manutahi** pā south Taranaki N.I.
**Maraenuku** pā Lower Hutt
**Massacre Hill** Tuamarina site Wairau Affray S.I.
**Matatā** Bay of Plenty N.I.
**Matawhero** Poverty Bay N.I.
**Mechanics Bay** Waitematā Harbour N.I.
**Meremere** bank Waikato River N.I.
**Meretoto** Ship Cove Marlborough Sds N.I.
**Mission Bay** Auckland N.I.
**Mōhaka** river & place eastern N.I.
**Mohua** Golden Bay top S.I.
**Mōtītī Island** Tauranga N.I.
**Motuarohia Island** Bay of Islands N.I.
**Moturoa** island & place New Plymouth N.I.
**Moutoa Island** upriver Whanganui N.I.
**Murihiku** Southland southernmost region S.I.
**Napier** Hawke's Bay eastern coast N.I.
**Nelson** top S.I.
**New Plymouth** Ngāmotu west coast Taranaki N.I.
**New South Wales** British colony Australia
**Ngāruawāhia** Waikato N.I.
**Ngātapa** west of Gisborne N.I.
**Northland** Auckland to top of N.I.
**Nu Tīreni** New Zealand
**Ōakura** near New Plymouth N.I.
**Oamaru** North Otago S.I.

**Ōhaeawai** Northland N.I.
**Ōhinemutu** Rotorua N.I.
**Ōkaiawa** south Taranaki N.I.
**Ōkaihau** Northland N.I.
**Okiato** Old Russell Bay of Islands N.I.
**Ōmarunui** Tūtaekuri River near Napier N.I.
**Onehunga** Auckland N.I.
**Onepoto** redoubt Waikaremoana N.I.
**Onukukaitara** northeast Taranaki N.I
**Ōpōtiki** eastern Bay of Plenty N.I.
**Ōrākau** near Kihikihi Waikato N.I.
**Ōtāhuhu** Auckland N.I.
**Ōtākou** Otago region south S.I.
**Ōtepoti** Dunedin southeast coast S.I.
**Ōtorohanga** King Country N.I.
**Otuataua** Māngere Auckland N.I.
**Ōtuihu** pā coastal Bay of Islands N.I.
**Oweta** pā Gisborne N.I.
**Paihia** near Waitangi N.I.
**Pākaraka** (ex Maxwell) Whanganui N.I.
**Panmure** Auckland N.I.
**Paremata** coast north of Wellington N.I.
**Parihaka** Taranaki N.I.
**Pātea** south Taranaki N.I.
**Paterangi** near Te Awamutu Waikato N.I.
**Patutahi** near Gisborne northeast N.I.
**Pāuatahanui** by Paremata N.I.
**Pipiriki** at Whanganui River N.I.
**Pirongia** Alexandra Waikato N.I.
**Pokino** Pōkeno Waikato N.I.
**Polynesia** east Pacific islands
**Port Cooper** Lyttelton Harbour S.I.
**Port Levy** harbour Banks Peninsula S.I.
**Pōterīwhi** pā Tauranga harbour N.I.
**Poverty Bay** east coast south Gisborne N.I.
**Pukekohe** south Auckland N.I.
**Pukerangiora** Waitara River Taranaki N.I.
**Puketakauere** northeast Taranaki N.I.
**Puniu River** Waipa tributary N.I.
**Pūtiki** pā across river from Whanganui N.I.
**Queen's Redoubt** Pōkeno Waikato N.I.
**Raglan** Whāingaroa west coast Waikato N.I.
**Rangiaowhia** by Te Awamutu Waikato N.I.
**Rangihoua** northwest shore Bay of Islands
**Rangiriri** Waikato River near Lake Waikare N.I.
**Rangitīkei** southwest north Wellington N.I.
**Rātana** near Whanganui N.I.
**Raukawa** Cook Strait between N.I & S.I.
**Rawene** Hokianga Harbour N.I.
**Remuera** Auckland N.I.
**Rotorua** lake & place Bay of Plenty N.I.
**Ruapekapeka** pā southeast Northland N.I.
**Ruatāhuna** Te Urewera N.I.
**Rūātoki** eastern Bay of Plenty N.I.
**Sentry Hill** Te Morere Taranaki N.I.
**Stewart Island** Rakiura south of S.I.
**Sumner** coastal Christchurch S.I.
**Sydney** city NSW Australia
**Tahiti** large Polynesian island
**Takahue** Far North N.I.
**Tapapa** east Waikato N.I.
**Taranaki** mt & area west N.I.
**Taupiri Mt** Taupiri Range Waikato N.I.
**Taupō** near centre of N.I.
**Tauranga** coast western Bay of Plenty N.I.
**Taurangaika** pā south Taranaki N.I.
**Taurangamirumiru** pā Waikato N.I.
**Te Ahuahu** volcanic peak Northland N.I.
**Te Ao Mārama** near Ōmārama S.I.
**Te Awamutu** south of Hamilton Waikato N.I.
**Te Ika-a-Māui** N.I. (fish of Māui)
**Te Kapotai** pā Bay of Islands N.I.
**Te Kohia** pā on disputed land Taranaki N.I.
**Te Kopani** shore of Lake Waikaremoana N.I.
**Te Kuiti** King Country N.I.
**Te Kurī-a-Pāoa** Young Nicks Head, N.I.
**Te Moana-nui-a-Kiwa** Pacific (great sea of Kiwa)
**Te Mōrere** Sentry Hill Waiongona R Taranaki N.I.
**Te Ngutu-o-te-manu** south Taranaki N.I.
**Te Papa** Tauranga Bay of Plenty N.I.
**Te Pōrere** near Tongariro N.I.
**Te Putere** Bay of Plenty coast N.I.
**Te Ranga** Tauranga N.I.
**Te Rou Rangatira** Te Tii site by Waitangi N.I.
**Te Teko** Rangitaiki River Bay of Plenty N.I.
**Te Teoteo** pā on ridge by Waikato R N.I.
**Te Tii** marae by Waitangi River N.I.
**Te Urewera** near East Coast N.I.
**Te Wai Pounamu** S.I. (waters of greenstone)
**Te Whata-a-pona** pā Te Urewera N.I.
**Tokerau** beach Northland N.I.
**Tongariro** Taupō volcanic zone N.I.
**Tory Channel** Marlborough S.I.
**Tuamarina** stream tributary Wairau R S.I.
**Tūranga** Gisborne east coast N.I.
**Tūranganganui-a-kiwa** Poverty Bay N.I.
**Turuturumōkai** near Hāwera Taranaki N.I.
**Tūtaekurī** river Hawke's Bay N.I.
**United Nations** Headquarters in New York
**Waahi** on banks Waikato River N.I.
**Waerenga-a-Hika** pā by Gisborne N.I.
**Waiāri** pā Mangapiko River Waikato N.I.
**Waikare** inlet Northland bay N.I.
**Waikato** river & region south of Auckland N.I.
**Waimana Valley** northern Urewera N.I.
**Waimate North** Northland N.I.
**Waimate plain** south Taranaki N.I.
**Waingongoro River** Taranaki N.I.
**Waipā R** tributary Waikato R N.I.
**Wairau** river & valley & plain Marlborough S.I.
**Waireka** hill near New Plymouth Taranaki N.I.
**Wairoa R** Tauranga N.I.
**Waitaki Valley** east coast Otago S.I.
**Waitangi** Bay of Islands N.I.
**Waitara Valley** north Taranaki N.I.
**Waitematā** Auckland harbour N.I.
**Wellington** by southernmost point N.I.
**Weroroa** pā Waitōtara River N.I.
**Whakatāne** eastern Bay of Plenty N.I.
**Whanganui** river & place west coast N.I.
**Wharekauri** Chathams east of S.I.
**Whareongaonga** east coast south of Gisborne N.I.


PHOTOCOPYING OF THIS PAGE IS RESTRICTED UNDER LAW.
ISBN: 9780170462419